Moments

THE PULITZER PRIZE PHOTOGRAPHS

A VISUAL CHRONICLE OF OUR TIME

TEXT BY HAL BUELL

WITH A FOREWORD BY SEYMOUR TOPPING

KÖNEMANN

For Regan and William Radcliffe. Know the past, see the future.

Designed by Dutton & Sherman Design

First published by Black Dog & Leventhal Publishers, Inc.
151 West 19th Street
New York, N.Y. 10011

Copyright © 2000 of this edition
Könemann Verlagsgesellschaft mbH
Bonner Strasse 126, D-Cologne 50968

Production: Ursula Schümer
Printing and Binding: Kossuth Printing House Co., Budapest

Printed in Hungary

ISBN 3-8290-3598-5

10 9 8 7 6 5 4 3 2 1

Contents

Foreword

For most people, images have supplanted print and radio as the prime means of observing the parade of news events. Television pours forth a daily tide of images that washes over us leaving only a very few in our memory. It remains for the photojournalist to provide the lasting images that are the benchmarks of our lives. No collection of photographs serves the historical record better than the group of pictures that, since 1942, have won the Pulitzer Prize for photography.

These photographs typically bear witness to courage, as in Joe Rosenthal's 1945 image of marines raising the flag over Iwo Jima; or to national shock, in Bob Jackson's 1963 picture of the shooting of Lee Harvey Oswald; or to compassion, in Moneta Sleet, Jr.'s 1968 portrait of Coretta Scott King at the funeral of her murdered husband; or to an appeal to conscience of people everywhere in Kevin Carter's 1993 photo of the starving Sudanese refugee child trailed by a vulture.

Each March, thirteen juries of eminent journalists and academics assemble in New York at Columbia University's Graduate School of Journalism to nominate finalists in the Pulitzer newspaper competition. Normally, they will scrutinize more than 1,400 entries, including about 150 in photography submitted either as individual images or in a portfolio form. The juries make three nominations in each of fourteen categories; the photography jury of five editors and photographers offers nominations in the two categories of spot news photography and feature photography. These nominations are reviewed by the Pulitzer Prize Board, composed of nineteen leading journalists and academics, which selects the winners at a meeting in April.

The independent Pulitzer Board derives its authority and its original endowment from the 1904 will of Joseph Pulitzer, publisher of the *New York World* and the *St. Louis Post-Dispatch*. Of an endowment to Columbia University of $2,000,000 for the establishment of a School of Journalism, one-fourth was "applied to prizes or scholarships for the encouragement of public service, public morals, American literature, and the advancement of education." Over the years, the categories of prizes, which were first awarded in 1917, have been expanded to twenty-one awards and modified by successive boards in keeping with the evolutionary changes in journalism, letters, music, and drama. A prize for photography was established in 1942, and in 1968 that category was divided into two—one for spot news photography and one for feature photography. There is every reason to believe that Joseph Pulitzer would have been delighted by the Board decision to make awards in photography, for he was the first publisher to make extensive use of newspaper illustrations. As recorded by James Barrett, the last editor of *The World*, Pulitzer told a group of journalists in 1902:

> They call me the father of illustrated journalism. What folly! I never thought of any such thing. I had a small newspaper which had been dead for years, and I was trying in every way to build up its circulation. What could I use for bait? A picture of course. On page one, in a position that would make *The World* stand out as the paper lay folded on the newsstand...a picture of someone prominent in the news of the day. There was a talented Russian artist in New York with a real genius for making portraits—Valerian Gribayedoff. Could he, with a photograph for model, draw a portrait so that it could be printed in the *World?* He could. Next day and every day thereafter, we showed on the upper-right hand section of our first page the picture of a statesman, a blushing bride, a fugitive absconder, or a murderer on occasion—whoever was most prominent in the day's doings. Circulation grew by the thousands.

That was a day, of course, when halftone engravings were not yet developed and editors had to rely on cut lines for illustrations. Already, Pulitzer was pointing the way toward modern newspaper photography. One can speculate that the innovative Pulitzer might have been inclined earlier than the Board to establish a photography prize category. It was only with the entry of the United States into World War II that the Board responded to the American public's intense interest in newspaper photographs that depicted graphically the travails of their soldiers in action. In 1944, Frank Filan, of the Associated Press, won the prize for his coverage of the bloody struggle for the Pacific island of Tarawa. Pulitzer recognition thereafter often went to the combat photographers in action in the Korean war and in Vietnam, and more recently in ethnic and regional conflicts worldwide.

Most authorities agree that Joseph Pulitzer's dream has been realized in terms of the impact the prizes he instituted have made on American life. They have served as an incentive to quality performance and to the raising of standards. Judging photographs was made more complex by the introduction of color photography in the 1970s. In black-and-white, there was a unique and established discipline. The introduction of color tempted some editors to decorate their news pages, rather than give uncompromising priority to the substance of photographs and their news value. In its adherence to standards in photography, the Board has also firmly resisted the increasingly common practice of computer manipulation. The board's Plan of Award state that "no entry whose content is manipulated or altered, apart from standard newspaper cropping and editing, will be deemed acceptable."

That the Pulitzer competition continues to reward substance can be seen in the 1997 winners. In the spot news category, Annie Wells, of the *Press Democrat* of Santa Rosa, California, received the award for her photograph of a firefighter rescuing a young girl from a rampaging river. There were photographs from all over the world in stunning color in that competition, but the jurors looked to a rural corner of California and a picture that celebrated the courage of a firefighter and the work that others like him do. In feature photography, Alexander Zemlianichenko, of Associated Press, won for his photograph of Russian President Boris Yeltsin dancing at a rock concert during his campaign for re-election. It was a colorful and funny photo, but it also demonstrated Russia's progress toward democracy. Can you imagine Stalin or former President Brezhnev swinging for re-election at a jazz concert?

While the Pulitzer Prizes in photography are confined to photographs printed in an American newspaper, the competition evokes great interest abroad. The first comprehensive exhibition of prize-winning photographs opened in 1998 in Tokyo's Bunkumara Museum. Staged by the Nippon Television Network in cooperation with the Pulitzer Board, the exhibition attracted 515,000 visitors during its year-long tour. The Japan exhibition inspired subsequent touring exhibitions in South Korea, Taiwan, and the United States.

Photography contributes to universal understanding, both intrinsically and illustratively. The Pulitzer Board quite often has been so impressed by the manner in which a story submitted in a print category has been brought alive by illustrative photos printed with it that it has been compelled to divide the awards between the nominated writers and photographers involved. In 1997, the prize for explanatory journalism went to Michael Vitez, reporter, and April Saul and Ron Cortes, photographers, of the *Philadelphia Inquirer*, for a series of stories on the choices that confront critically ill patients who sought to die with dignity. Also, photographers often are counted among the winners in the category of Public Service by a newspaper and other staff awards.

The crowning achievement for a photographer remains an award in the spot news or feature categories. In 1999, the actual prize was a citation and a check for $5,000. This amount seems small compared to some other major awards, but a Pulitzer Prize brings recognition beyond any other award in the field. The winner makes a distinctive contribution to the historical record and, in doing so, becomes a part of it.

—Seymour Topping

1942

Labor Strife in Detroit

BY MILTON BROOKS, *THE DETROIT NEWS*

In the 1940s and 1950s, before motor drives could feed film through a camera at five frames per second, patience was as much the photographer's tool as was the camera. The cumbersome operation of the Speed Graphic camera meant that photographers could only shoot one frame every six or seven seconds. Yet pictures, as every cameraman working on the street knew, came and went with the blink of an eye.

In the spring of 1941, Milton Brooks's photographic attention was not focused on the war in Europe, or on the growing troubles with Japan. Instead, he was in Detroit, at one of Ford Motor Company's biggest plants, the River Rouge, where labor trouble was brewing. Brooks, who was called "One-shot Milton," was a master of patience. In Detroit photography circles, it was said that he would wait until the right picture was about to happen, make one shot, and then go home.

Never before had a Ford plant in Detroit been closed by a strike; Henry Ford always insisted that he would close a plant before he would deal with the unions. Times were changing, however, and years of violence had characterized much union activity as labor won its franchise in the streets. General Motors had caved in to the union, as had Chrysler. Still, Henry Ford could not bear the idea of negotiation.

On April 3, inside the River Rouge plant, a worker was fired, and the cry "strike" was heard throughout the grounds. Striking workers walked the line, urging nonstrikers to walk out. The 120,000-man plant was closed down. Strikebreakers and unionists clashed.

Milton Brooks was patient, as he always was; and watching for the right moment, he noticed a man arguing with a group of pickets. Brooks later recalled, "He had the wrong side of the argument, and I knew there would be trouble pretty soon." Other photographers moved on to look for scenes with more graphic interest than a verbal exchange, but Brooks waited.

The man arguing with the pickets tried to push his way through the line. The strikers stiffened their positions. The clubs came out, and Brooks moved forward; the man attempted to protect himself, but the clubs swung and the ever-patient Brooks unobtrusively made the picture.

His photograph was awarded the first-ever Pulitzer Prize for photography.

MAY **1941** ■ *Rudolf Hess makes a mysterious trip to Scotland, where his plane crash lands.*

MAY ■ *Orson Welles's film* Citizen Kane *opens.*

OCTOBER ■ *Joe DiMaggio hits safely in 56 consecutive games, establishing a major league record.*

DECEMBER ■ *Japan bombs Pearl Harbor. President Roosevelt declares December 7, 1941 a date "which will live in infamy."*

TECHNICAL DETAILS CAMERA 4x5 Speed Graphic
FILM Kodak
LENS 127 mm
SHUTTER & APERTURE Unknown

A Hero Returns

BY EARLE BUNKER, *THE OMAHA WORLD-HERALD*

In 1943, Villisca, Iowa was a hamlet of 1,100 people about 50 miles southeast of Omaha, nearly lost on the great prairies that sweep across America west of Chicago. On a road map, Villisca rated just one type size larger than the names of the smallest of villages; it was the essence of small-town America, a town that recognized it heroes.

On July 15, 1943, Lt. Col. Robert Moore returned to Villisca from a distant war. The *Omaha World-Herald* assigned Earle Bunker to cover the story because Moore was a hero, the real thing. Here was a chance for him to make a picture about the war that would be different than the depictions of combat bullfire that filled the news pages in the early 1940s, a chance to reveal the depth of emotion the war stirred in families throughout the country.

Moore *was* a real hero. He and his fellow Iowans had faced off against Germany's Desert Fox, Field Marshal Rommel, and his rugged Panzers in North Africa. Moore and his battalion held off two Panzer divisions on a hill called Lessouda until his outfit was ordered to withdraw.

That did not end the fighting, however. The U.S. troops were 15 miles behind German lines, and as Moore led his men through the enemy positions, they faced machine-gun, artillery, and sniper fire. Thirty-five members of the battalion fell before the German guns. The battalion finally reached Kasserine Pass in Tunisia, but German bombing caught up with them and Moore was wounded. He was awarded the Distinguished Service Cross for his heroic leadership and then ordered home.

Villisca is a long way from Tobruk, Tripoli, and Casablanca, names that would become memories, but in 1943 those names were all too real. Earle Bunker waited for some twenty-four hours for the train carrying the hero home to his wife, Dorothy, and their seven-year-old daughter, Nancy, and the patient, jubilant town population.

When the train rolled into the small Villisca station, the soldier, who had been away for sixteen months, stepped out, saw Nancy, and dropped his baggage and equipment. The child rushed from the crowd and was enveloped by her father's arms, while Dorothy Moore covered her face with her hands.

Bunker carefully chose his moment and captured a scene as timeless as life itself—a hero coming home to family, love, and a way of life.

TECHNICAL DETAILS   **CAMERA** 4x5 Speed Graphic
    FILM Kodak
    LENS 127 mm
    SHUTTER & APERTURE Unknown

The Iwo Jima Flag

BY JOE ROSENTHAL, ASSOCIATED PRESS

On February 19, 1945, as the landing craft bounced and swayed through the sea toward Iwo Jima, AP staff photographer Joe Rosenthal and his U.S. Marine companions could see their destination—the black sands of the beach and, in the background, Mount Suribachi, a brooding watchtower that commanded a view of the entire island.

The coming days would expose all of them to vicious fighting. Rosenthal knew he would photograph a fierce battle, since all the Pacific Island battles had been fierce; but he didn't know that Iwo Jima would be the site of the bloodiest battle in Marine Corps history. He had no way to foresee that, in several days, he would be atop Suribachi, where he would take the most famous photograph of World War II and arguably the greatest American photo icon in history. And win a Pulitzer Prize.

As the landing craft struck the Iwo beach with a crunch, Rosenthal took his first pictures of Marines dashing toward what little cover there was on the beach. He ran for cover himself as he scrambled to photograph the battle. Marines fell around him, caught in the enemy crossfire. "No one knows how they survived that beach," he says. "It was like walking in rain without getting hit."

Iwo Jima (translated, "sulphur island") was a Japanese home island, actually a part of Tokyo, but some 700 miles distant. In the millenia of the nation's history, foreign troops had never invaded Japan's home territory. The American military leaders knew the impact of a landing on Iwo Jima would be devastating to the morale and intensely nationalistic pride of the Japanese.

Some 70,000 troops—50,000 Americans and 22,000 Japanese—met head to head on Iwo Jima's eight square miles. In the month-long battle, close to 40 percent would die, nearly 7,000 Americans and more than 20,000 of the Japanese garrison.

Joe Rosenthal covered the fighting daily, shipping packets of film back to Guam by air. Editors sorted them and transmitted the best images immediately via radiophoto to San Francisco, where they were transmitted to the rest of the world. His dramatic pictures of the Iwo Jima landings won spectacular play in newspapers and magazines.

Five days after landing, Rosenthal heard that a platoon of Marines would ascend Mount Suribachi and raise a flag. He gathered his equipment and prepared to transfer to a landing craft from the command ship just off shore, where he had gone to photograph Navy Secretary James Forrestal. He tossed his cameras to a colleague; but as he turned to step onto the smaller vessel, he slipped and plunged into the rolling sea. The sides of the ships hovered above him, and he thought, as he watched the tillerman fiercely spinning the wheel, I sure hope he gets it right. The seaman did, the vessels moved apart, and Rosenthal was pulled from the water. Once on shore, he replaced the helmet he lost in the incident and

MAY **1944** ▪ *Jean-Paul Sartre's play* No Exit *is performed in Paris. His novel* Being and Nothingness *was published in 1943.*

JUNE ▪ *D-day landings begin on the beaches of Normandy.*

AUGUST ▪ *The Allies liberate Paris.*

The Winecoff Hotel Fire

BY ARNOLD HARDY, ASSOCIATED PRESS

For Georgia Tech student Arnold Hardy, Friday nights were an opportunity to go dancing and stay out late. Arriving home in the wee hours of the morning on December 7, 1946, Hardy heard the sirens of fire engines. He called the fire department and learned that Atlanta's Winecoff Hotel, on Peachtree Street, was ablaze.

Hardy, an amateur photographer, grabbed his brand-new 2 1/4 by 3 1/4 Speed Graphic (slightly smaller than the classic 4x5), a film pack, and his entire cache of five flash bulbs. A cab took him to within two blocks of the hotel, and he ran the rest of the way. He turned a corner and, at 4:15 a.m., stopped short in his tracks. "Rounding the corner, I came upon it all at once. Fire was raging from the upper floors. From almost every window men, women, and children screamed for help," he said later.

Newspapers recounted the horror in detail. A peculiarity in the Atlanta building code allowed the structure, built in 1913, to be constructed without fire escapes. The fire flashed through hallways and stairways, preventing escape from within the building. Only the windows provided a way out.

Fire ladders could only reach the ninth floor of the fifteen-floor structure. Hotel guests tried to escape from upper floors by using bed sheets tied together to descend to the ladders, but the sheets tore or pulled apart and bodies fell to the pavement. Some guests tried to creep along the ledge from window to window and slipped, falling to the street. One woman threw her two children from a window, despite the call of the firemen to wait until nets were ready. She then followed, and all three died. Another woman jumped and crashed into a fireman who was helping a guest escape on a ladder below; the three plunged to the street. A narrow alley behind the hotel became piled deep with the bodies of those who fell trying to leap a ten-foot space between the hotel and a neighboring building.

Hardy made a few pictures as he watched the scene in horror. "Suddenly," he says, "I heard someone shriek. I looked up, raising my camera. A woman was plummeting downward. As she passed the third floor, I fired, using my last flashbulb." The falling woman hit a pipe that held the marquee, then bounced into a railing around the marquee and onto the street. As forceful as each collision was, they broke her fall and she lived.

But 118 others of the 256 guests did not. Many of the survivors on the upper floors were those wise enough to block the cracks around the doors to stop the smoke and await rescue. The owner, W. F. Winecoff, was found dead in his fourteenth floor suite alongside his wife, who also perished.

Hardy developed his pictures and hurried them in a wet towel to the offices of the Associated Press in Atlanta. Three of his pictures were transmitted to the world. His Pulitzer was the first prize awarded to an amateur.

TECHNICAL DETAILS   CAMERA 2 x 3 Speed Graphic
FILM Kodak film pack
LENS 100 mm
SHUTTER & APERTURE Flash @ f4.5

MARCH **1946** ▪ *Winston Churchill gives his "iron curtain" speech in Fulton, Missouri.*

JULY ▪ *Mother Frances Cabrini, the first American saint, is canonized.*

OCTOBER ▪ *Goering, Hess, Ribbentrop and others are convicted at the Nuremberg war crimes trial. Nine of the convicted criminals are executed.*

DECEMBER ▪ *The film* It's a Wonderful Life, *starring Jimmy Stewart, is released.*

A Boy, A Pistol, and Trouble

BY FRANK CUSHING, *THE BOSTON HERALD*

On a lazy early-summer afternoon in June 1947, *Boston Herald* photographer Frank Cushing was sitting in his radio car outside a Howard Johnson restaurant, waiting to photograph victims of a two-bit holdup. The story was so routine, he knew that the photograph might not even make the paper.

Then Cushing heard the crackled sounds of an alert coming from the radio of a police car parked alongside his vehicle. A shooting had taken place…an officer was injured…a hostage was held…and it was just down the street. Cushing shifted into gear and sped to the scene.

Two police officers had stopped a fifteen-year-old youth and questioned him about a robbery. Suddenly the boy, Ed Bancroft, pulled out a pistol and started shooting. He wounded one policeman in the arm and fled into a nearby alley, where he grabbed a hostage, another fifteen-year-old named Bill Ronan.

The cops quickly blocked the ends of the alley to cut off Bancroft's escape, but he threatened to shoot Ronan if the police came closer. He fired several times at police and repeatedly shoved the gun into Ronan's back.

Cushing managed to make a long shot from the end of the alley, but he knew it would be a bad photo because he was too far away.

Events began to move quickly. The police began to move closer, and Bancroft once again screamed his threat to shoot Ronan. He shot at the police as they moved in.

Meanwhile, Cushing went out to the street and calculated which house was across the alley from where the two youths were positioned. He talked the owner into letting him in, crept along a sun porch, and—very, very carefully—made his picture of the two boys. "I was wondering whether the kid would shoot me," Cushing said later. "But I wanted that picture."

By this time, there were about thirty policemen in the area. One of them worked his way along the fence to a spot where Bancroft was making his stand and trying to figure a way out. At the right moment, the cop stood up behind Bancroft, reached over the fence, and stunned him with the butt of a weapon. The dazed youth, who had nothing to do with the Howard Johnson robbery, was taken into custody immediately and jailed.

Cushing's photograph was remarkable because at a time when hostage situations were rare, his photograph showed one actually underway. In addition, the limited lens capabilities of the Speed Graphic, the usual camera of the press photographer, meant that cameramen had to be close to their subjects, which is generally not possible in a hostage situation. Cushing's ingenuity and persistence paid off and resulted in an extraordinary picture.

JANUARY **1947** ▪ *Chicago gangster Al Capone dies.*

APRIL ▪ *Jackie Robinson signs with the Brooklyn Dodgers, becoming the first black baseball player in the major leagues.*

OCTOBER ▪ *Hollywood visits Washington D.C. to protest the House Un-American Activities Committee hearings.*

OCTOBER ▪ *The first 300 families move into Levittown, on Long Island, New York, which was constructed to satisfy post-war housing demands.*

TECHNICAL DETAILS   **CAMERA** 4x5 Speed Graphic
FILM Kodak
LENS 127 mm
SHUTTER & APERTURE Unknown

1949

The Babe Bows Out

BY NAT FEIN, *THE NEW YORK HERALD TRIBUNE*

Some photographs transcend their subjects. They are images whose meaning grows with time; they mark not just a special place, but a special era. They remind us of much more than the moment in time they depict. These pictures become icons.

Nat Fein, of the *New York Herald Tribune,* made such an icon when he was assigned to Yankee Stadium to photograph the last appearance of George Herman Ruth, the mighty Babe, the Sultan of Swat, the King of Clout. It was June 13, 1948, a dreary, bleak day.

The Babe was very ill and had not played baseball in some fifteen years, but memories of the years when he did play drew a packed house. The fans were there to say farewell, and Ruth was for everything.

Fein knew that Ruth's uniform, number three, would be retired. As The Babe accepted the cheers of the assembled multitude, Fein positioned himself behind Ruth and photographed the number as well as the man.

No caption was needed for the photograph. The shoulders, stooped slightly by illness, were nevertheless the mighty shoulders of the great home-run hitter. The spindly legs were those that carried Ruth around the bases in his trademark jog. The heavy head of hair was also recognizable from the rear. Ruth leaned on his bat, using it as a kind of cane to steady himself as the crowd's tribute flowed over him. Fein opened his lens wide and shot at a slow shutter speed without a flash. The out-of-focus background that resulted highlighted the Babe and his pinstripe uniform.

The event was Ruth's formal good-bye to baseball, but the farewell picture said good-bye to much more—to a special time in sports, or maybe just to a special time. One writer called it a golden age that was a lazy afternoon in the nation's history, a baseball afternoon. And a Golden Age of sports. Jack Dempsey. Bobby Jones. Red Grange. Paavo Nurmi. Lou Gehrig. Jesse Owens. Joe Louis.

It's true that the Babe caroused. He trained on hot dogs and beer and maybe spent too much time with the ladies; but he hit homers, sometimes on demand. He had a ready pen for the kids, and he brought great excitement to many a summer afternoon. He left a string of records that lasted for years. Even when he struck out he did it with class.

Babe Ruth died two months after Nat Fein took his picture. The man named Babe died, but not the legend named Babe.

TECHNICAL DETAILS   **CAMERA** 4x5 Speed Graphic
FILM Kodak
LENS 5 inch
SHUTTER & APERTURE 1/100th @ f5.6

Close Call

BY BILL CROUCH, *THE OAKLAND TRIBUNE*

Chet Derby made his living as a crop duster. He flew his biplane over Northern California farmland, dodging telephone wires, power lines, and big trees. He earned extra income by performing in his plane at air shows, which provided a popular postwar Sunday afternoon entertainment. The spectators got to see the old war planes and watch them fly over, and pilots like Derby performed stunts: loop-the-loop, wing walkers, flying low over the field.

The *Oakland Tribune's* Bill Crouch, himself a pilot, surveyed the 60,000 air-show fans enjoying a crisp October day at the Oakland Airport as he looked for a good spot from which to photograph the aerial show.

Derby's performance was to culminate in his hottest stunt. Trailing smoke from his agile biplane, he would do an upside-down loop-the-loop, leaving large smoky circles in the sky.

One minute after he finished, three B-29 bombers were sup-posed to come roaring overhead in formation, each a shimmering silver bird with all four engines at full power.

As Derby was flying, twisting, and turning, doing his stuff, Crouch was trying to get an artistic shot that combined Derby's plane with the smoke circles against the blue sky. He bent this way and that, and finally settled on what looked like the correct perspective.

All of a sudden, one minute early, the bombers roared across the airport. Derby, upside down as his stunt proscribed, didn't see them coming. Crouch aimed his camera at the sky. Later he commented, "I was concentrating on shooting pictures of the stunt plane. I saw the bombers flying in and thought it might make a different picture with them in the shot." And then he added, in what is a classic of understatement, "It sure did."

The bomber's wing missed Derby's plane by five feet.

JANUARY **1949** ■ *Mao takes Beijing, proclaims the People's Republic of China.*

MAY ■ *Arthur Miller's play* Death of a Salesman *wins the Pulitzer Prize.*

DECEMBER ■ *Katherine Hepburn and Spencer Tracy appear together in the movie* Adam's Rib.

TECHNICAL DETAILS CAMERA 4x5 Speed Graphic
FILM Kodak
LENS Unknown
SHUTTER & APERTURE Unknown

1952

Johnny Bright Sacked

BY DON ULTANG AND JOHN ROBINSON, *THE DES MOINES REGISTER*

On Saturday, October 21, 1951, Des Moines' Drake University was visiting Oklahoma A&M. The Drake team was led by Johnny Bright, probably the best halfback in college football. For three seasons, he rushed for more yardage than any other player; and, in the previous season, 1950, he averaged 266 yards per game.

Bright was different from other college players of the time in one important way, he was black; in the early 1950s, black players were not welcome on the gridiron of big-time college football.

Don Ultang and John Robinson were assigned to the game by the *Des Moines Register,* which covered all the big games involving Iowa teams. They had been experimenting with motion picture equipment, as well as other special cameras, to improve coverage by shooting photo sequences that followed the step-by-step progress of key plays in a game.

Oklahoma A&M kicked off to Drake. Drake had the ball on Oklahoma's thirty-yard line for the first play of the game. Bright got the ball from center and handed it off to the fullback, who headed for a hole in the line. Well back of scrimmage, Bright watched the play evolve. Then, WHACK, he was hit full-force by A&M defensive back Wilbanks Smith, who ignored the fullback but blindsided Bright long after he had handed off the ball.

Smith smacked Bright with his fist and forearm and broke his jaw. Bright was knocked out, but he recovered quickly and got back on his feet. Despite the broken jaw, a wobbly Bright took the ball from center on the next play and threw a long pass for a touchdown. The large contingent of Drake fans went wild.

Oklahoma took the subsequent kickoff, but quickly punted, giving Drake the ball again. On the third Drake play of the game, Bright took the pass from center, and handed the ball off. Once again, ten yards away from the ball carrier, Wilbanks Smith hit Bright, knocking him down. Incredibly, Bright got up; and on the next play, he ran the ball himself. He was hit hard and knocked down; this time he stayed down and had to be carried off the field.

Thanks to their careful planning and high-speed sequence photography, Ultang and Robinson captured the chain of events on film. Using a motion picture camera, Robinson shot a picture series that showed the step-by-step development of the play. Ultang's photo, made with a Speed Graphic and a twenty-inch lens, caught the actual blow (see the upper right corner of both photos).Together, the photos documented how far Bright was out of the play action when Smith hit him. The pictures appeared that Sunday and in subsequent editions of the *Des Moines Register,* and they were picked up by the wire services and transmitted everywhere.

In the controversy that ensued, Oklahoma claimed it was an accident; Drake claimed it was not. Arguments flew back and forth between the schools, and Drake complained about the lack of resolution to the situation and withdrew from the conference for a while.

Bright went on to play successful professional football in Canada. The Ultang/Robinson photos remain testimony to Johnny Bright's courage and to a time when it wasn't that easy for a black football player to take the field on an autumn afternoon.

MARCH 1951 ▪ *Julius and Ethel Rosenberg are convicted of wartime espionage.*

APRIL ▪ *General Douglas MacArthur receives a triumphal welcome at a joint meeting of Congress.*

JUNE ▪ *British spies Guy Burgess and Donald MacLean flee to Moscow; British double-agent Kim Philby has told them that their cover was blown.*

OCTOBER ▪ *I Love Lucy, starring Lucille Ball and Desi Arnez, begins its long run on television.*

TECHNICAL DETAILS   **CAMERA** 35 mm motion picture adapted to sequence still
FILM 4x5 Speed Graphic
LENS 20 inch lens on Speed Graphic
SHUTTER & APERTURE Unknown

Trucker's Rescue

BY VIRGINIA SCHAU, AMATEUR

The countryside along the highway from Los Angeles to Portland is a traveler's delight. Some of the scenery, especially farther north, is lovely if you are an outdoor-lover on a fishing trip, but truckers have their eyes focused on the center line, with occasional reference to highway route numbers and miles traveled. There may be a chance for a quick snooze in the cab while your partner takes a turn at the wheel.

On Sunday, May 3, 1953, Walter and Virginia Schau were out to try their luck on the opening day of the fishing season. Bud Overby and Hank Baum, trucking partners, were pushing for Portland with a load of radishes, carrots, and the season's first watermelon.

The Schaus slowed up behind the lumbering truck. The highway curved at a spot called Bailey Hill, some ten miles north of Redding, and the road's twists and turns prevented the Schaus from passing the slow-moving truck.

A few miles back, Baum had turned the wheel to Overby and was about to climb into the sleeper for a nap. As they rolled onto the Pitt River Bridge, a forty-foot-high structure that carried traffic over Lake Shasta, the truck suddenly lost its steering, swerved, and hit the curb of the bridge. Accompanied by the sound of screeching and tearing metal, the truck tore through the guardrail and bounced over the side of the bridge.

There was a sudden jolt, and the cab stopped in midair. The two truckers were upside down, in a kind of crouch, on the wind- shield of the rig, looking down forty feet to the rocky shoreline of the lake. By some miracle, the wheels of the cab became entangled under the trailer; and the cab and its occupants were suspended in space, swaying ever so slightly.

From their car behind the truck, Walter and Virginia Schau watched horrified as the accident ran its course in front of them. They pulled up behind the truck and asked other drivers, now stopped on the elevated highway, whether they were carrying any rope. One motorist had a length of marine line, and Walter called down to the drivers, "We have some rope. We'll throw it down to you and try to haul you out."

The rope came down and Overby next to the window grabbed it. He was the first out. "I'll get it back to you as soon as I can," he told his partner. As Overby was pulled up, Baum began to smell the acrid odor of burning diesel fuel. Smoke began to enter the cabin, and he crawled halfway out the window to escape the fumes. Down came the rope again, and he was hauled up. Atop the bridge, the two men embraced and exclaimed about how fortunate they were to have survived. As if to emphasize the point, the then-burning cab broke loose from the trailer and crashed to the rocks below.

During the course of the rescue, Virginia Schau grabbed her Brownie camera from the back of the car. She recalled that the film had been in the camera for more than a year, but she knew there were frames still unexposed. She ran to a knoll across from the bridge and

took pictures of the rescue. A professional photographer would say that it was the wrong camera, the wrong lens, and the wrong film, but those same professionals would also admit the importance of being at the right place at the right time—with any camera. The photo was so dramatic that it won the Pulitzer Prize; it was the first Pulitzer photo to be made with a camera other than a Speed Graphic. In addition, it was the first Pulitzer awarded to a woman; it would be another 32 years before the award was given to a female professional.

TECHNICAL DETAILS   CAMERA Kodak Box Brownie
FILM Kodak
LENS Bownie lens with standard focal length
SHUTTER & APERTURE Standard Brownie

1959

The Little Red Wagon and Death

BY WILLIAM SEAMAN, *THE MINNEAPOLIS STAR-TRIBUNE*

In the 1950s, city newspapers assigned photographers to radio cars. Like the police, the photographers patrolled the streets, listening to the tempo of city life on the police radio and responding to news breaks, mostly crimes and fires.

Bill Seaman, of the *Minneapolis Star-Tribune,* drove his radio car through the city about noon on a sunny day in mid-May, alert for stories. Several blocks behind him a garbage truck moved along noisily doing its job.

At the intersection of Riverside Drive and South Twenty-Seventh Street Seaman stopped for a red light. As he waited, a young boy, about the age of Seaman's young son, stepped into the intersection pulling a little red wagon.

Seaman recalled, "I was going to get out of the car and shout a warning to him to not cross, but he stepped back onto the sidewalk."

The light changed, and Seaman drove on. The garbage truck had moved forward to a block or so behind his car. Three blocks later, his police radio crackled out the bulletin that a small boy had been hit by a garbage truck at the intersection where he had just stopped. Seaman turned his radio car around, hoping against hope but fearing the worst. Fourteen people died in traffic fatalities that day, May 16; it was the worst day of 1958 for vehicular deaths.

Seaman, who spent 37 years as a photographer for the *Star-Tribune,* later recalled, "It was the most tragic photo I ever took." He retired in 1982 and continued to photograph for a while, but he later turned to painting, mostly subjects taken from pictures he made during his nearly four decades with the paper.

MARCH 1958 ■ *Nikita Khrushchev becomes chairman of the Soviet Council of Ministries, replacing Nikolai Bulganin.*

MAY ■ *China proclaims its great leap forward.*

JULY ■ *Americans buy 100 million Hula Hoops, manufactured by Wham-O, but the fad is short-lived.*

OCTOBER ■ *British Overseas Airways becomes the first airline to begin regular transatlantic service using jet passenger planes.*

TECHNICAL DETAILS   CAMERA Rolleiflex
FILM Kodak 120 roll film
LENS 80 mm
SHUTTER & APERTURE Unknown

1960

Execution at the Castle

BY ANDY LOPEZ, UNITED PRESS INTERNATIONAL

Cuba's San Severino Castle at Matanzas was a castle in every sense of the word. A moat surrounded the structure, and to gain entrance, visitors had to cross a bridge over the twenty-foot waterway. It had been a military base for President Fulgencio Batista's army; but after January 1, 1959, it was run by the *barbudos,* the bearded ones.

That was the nickname that Fidel Castro and his rebels were given by a joyful Cuban population that celebrated the fall of Havana and the ouster of Batista, who had fled the island, his party over. It was time for judgment.

Andy Lopez, a veteran New York-based photographer for United Press International, was on the scene at the castle on January, 17 to photograph Castro justice in action. Lopez, who preferred Yankee Stadium baseball as an assignment, was among those correspondents who flocked to Havana as Castro and his *barbudos* took over the capital.

"Anything you want," Castro told the journalists, and Lopez asked for and received credentials to cover the trial at the Matanzas castle. A Batista army corporal named Jose Rodriguez, but called Pepe Caliente (Hot Pete), was on trial for his brutal treatment of the populace. So great was the hatred for Pepe that hundreds of people pushed across the castle's bridge, some of them falling into the moat, to volunteer their testimony against him.

As Lopez recalls the trial, "It was noisy and unruly. There were lots of Coca-Cola bottles just thrown on the ground or floor during the proceedings. And on top of that, cigar butts. People walked on tables. The scene was incredible."

The prosecuting attorney was Willy Galvez. He was 25 years old and the commander of the Castro troops at San Severino. At one point, Lopez recalls, Galvez turned to Rodriguez and said, "When we get through with you, Pepe Caliente, they are going to call you Pepe Frio (Cold Pete)."

Galvez was true to his word. The trial, broadcast over a loud-speaker system to those assembled, lasted two hours, and Pepe was sentenced to death one minute later.

Lopez soon found himself in the courtyard of the castle with the condemned man and his squad of executioners. Rodriguez was put up against a wall, but a priest came forward. Rodriguez dropped to his knees before the priest, who administered the final sacrament. Pepe kissed a small crucifix and Lopez photographed the poignant moment, with the condemned man kneeling before the priest, the priest bent over, and the executioners in the background.

At that moment Galvez walked up to Lopez and told him, "No pictures." Lopez argued, and the *barbudos* began to get impatient. Galvez said he wanted the film; Lopez handed him a roll of film,

JANUARY **1959** ▪ *Rebel leader Fidel Castro takes Havana and becomes premier of Cuba.*

MARCH ▪ *Jack Lemmon, Tony Curtis, and Marilyn Monroe appear in Billy Wilder's* Some Like it Hot.

MARCH ▪ *Toy company Mattel, Inc. introduces the Barbie doll.*

JULY ▪ *U.S. President Nixon and Soviet Premier Khrushchev engage in a their famous Kitchen Cabinet debate in Moscow.*

but not THE film. He made a switch and gave Galvez a blank roll, keeping the onc with the picture on it, before Galvez sent the journalists away.

Lopez heard later that, at the last minute, Galvez stopped the execution, saying he needed higher authority. He got it, and the next day Rodriguez fell to a burst of gunfire in the courtyard.

TECHNICAL DETAILS   **CAMERA** Rolleiflex
FILM Kodak 120 roll film
LENS 80 mm
SHUTTER & APERTURE Unknown

critics was that all he ever attempted to do was to tell and show what happened as truthfully and fairly as possible. This was difficult. At one point, in a piece for an AP publication for staffers, he wrote about photographers who covered the fighting, citing the dangers and the limitations they encountered in Vietnam:

"They (photographers) could crawl to the forward trenches of a besieged outpost, wait beside riflemen in night ambushes, witness brutal interrogations and executions and merciless street fighting. While the enemy—the Vietcong and the North Vietnamese—operated in secrecy, American and allied troops and government civilians performed almost always under the probing eyes and lenses of newsmen."

Even though there was no censorship in Vietnam, Faas said he always tried to use judgment in his coverage. "We worked hard to be truthful. We avoided pictures of the bizarre and the atypical. But when torture became commonplace in the field, we photographed it and distributed the photos."

Faas's Pulitzer Prize for 1965 was the first Pulitzer of many to be awarded over the next decade to photographers and writers who faced the war with only cameras and notebooks as their shield against the battle.

At the end of his tour in Vietnam, he moved to London where he reported various stories in Europe and the Middle East, gradually moving toward an assignment to lead AP's picture operations in Europe, Africa, and the Middle East.

TECHNICAL DETAILS   **CAMERA** Leica
                         FILM Kodak
                         LENS Range from 35 mm to 200 mm
                         SHUTTER & APERTURE Various

While Faas was in Vietnam, many photographers from the AP as well as from other news companies were killed. Some died directly at the hands of Vietcong; others in aircraft or helicopter crashes. Seventeen newsmen disappeared into Cambodia. Many were Faas's friends, and all were his colleagues. In 1997, Faas and another Vietnam photographer, Tim Page, published a book titled *Requiem: By the Photographers Who Died in Vietnam and Indochina.* It included pictures taken by 135 photographers from both sides of the struggle who died during the 30 years of the French Indochina war and the American Vietnam war.

Meredith Shot on Highway 51

BY JACK THORNELL, ASSOCIATED PRESS

James Meredith was a man with a dream. His goal was to convince black citizens to register and vote in local and national elections. He believed that if he walked safely through the deepest part of the deep south he would see his dream become reality. Wearing a yellow pith helmet and carrying an ebony-and-ivory walking stick, Meredith planned to walk the 220 miles along U.S. Highway 51 from Memphis, Tennessee, to Jackson, Mississippi. In 1966, only 12,000 of some one million black citizens were registered in Mississippi.

Two years earlier the bodies of three civil rights workers, Andrew Goodman, Michael Schwerner, and James Chaney, who were on a similar voter registration mission, had been found dead near Philadelphia, Mississippi. The perfume of oak and honeysuckle offered regional charm and flavor, but Meredith's walk was no countryside stroll.

Everyone in Mississippi knew James Meredith. In 1962, with the help of the President of the United States, 538 U.S. marshals and 22,000 combat troops, he had integrated the University of Mississippi. After he left Ol' Miss, he spent time in Africa (the walking stick was the gift of a tribal chief) and studied law at Columbia University in New York.

Jack Thornell, from the Associated Press's New Orleans bureau, was assigned to cover the walk. He would stay with Meredith until relieved by another AP photographer several days later.

The story unfolded much as Thornell thought it might. Blacks along the way offered mute support, and many comments from whites were unfriendly. Some drove their cars and trucks too close, swerving as they came down the highway. One yelled, "I hope you die before you get there."

On the second day, Meredith and six companions—three blacks and three whites—walked along the steamy, muggy road in the kind of weather one might expect in June. Just south of the Mississippi line, Highway 51 took a long dip into a hollow. A black friend of Meredith ran up to say he had heard that a man with a gun was waiting for him down the highway.

All he could see coming down the road, though, was a black farmer with cool water. Meredith shrugged. Then a voice, ever so softly but nevertheless easily heard, said, "James. James. I only want James Meredith." Meredith looked in the direction of the call and saw a man in the brush along the roadway. The man leveled a shotgun at Meredith.

Thornell had parked his car a short distance ahead and was waiting for Meredith and his small group. At the first shot, he

---

APRIL **1966** ▪ *Mao Tse-tung launches the Cultural Revolution in China.*

JUNE ▪ *U.S. Supreme Court rules in Miranda v. Arizona that the police must advise anyone taken into custody that they have a right to counsel and to remain silent.*

SEPTEMBER ▪ *Science fiction television drama* Star Trek *premiers.*

OCTOBER ▪ *National Organization of Women is founded by Betty Friedan to help U.S. women gain equal rights.*

The Kiss of Life

BY ROCCO MORABITO, THE JACKSONVILLE (FLORIDA) *JOURNAL*

July 17, 1967, was a routine summer day in Florida; the heat was muggy and oppressing. It began as a routine day for pole linemen Randall Champion, Jimmy Thompson, and others of a crew that had been called out to restore power in a Jacksonville suburb where residents were complaining about the lack of air conditioning, and for *Journal* photographer Rocco Morabito, who had an assignment in the same suburb where the power was out.

On the way to his suburban assignment, Rocco saw the linemen atop their poles working on the problem. He made a mental note to stop on the way back to see if there might be a feature picture possibility in the work underway. As he completed his assignment, however, the situation with the power outage turned dramatic.

All the power lines were dead, except for one. As he worked high above the street, Champion somehow connected with the live wire and a twenty-one-hundred-volt surge of power coursed through his body, burned out through his feet, and knocked him from the pole. He was held by his safety harness, dangling upside down and unconscious. When Thompson and the others atop other poles saw what had happened, they knew that time was of the essence; the breath of life had to be pumped back into Champion's body.

Thompson was the first to reach Champion's pole. Up he went, grabbing his buddy's shoulders and head and starting CPR. When Morabito drove by enroute to his office, he could tell something was wrong, but didn't know what. He jumped out of his car, took a picture, and assessed the situation. He called his office on his car phone asking them to summon assistance; but unknown to him, a call for help had already been made.

Morabito returned to the scene and took more pictures. The other linemen watched intently for some sign of life as Thompson continued the CPR. He paused for an instant and called down, "He's breathing." By then, an ambulance was on the scene. Champion regained consciousness; he would be out of work for some time and his feet would need skin grafts where the electricity burned through, but he had survived.

Back at the *Journal,* Morabito processed his film. It was a little past the deadline, but the editor said he would hold it for the photo. Printed big on the front page, it was a positive photo that showed one human saving another, in stark contrast to the coverage of the Vietnam war, civil rights issues, and demonstrations in the streets that readers so often faced during this era.

JUNE 1967 ▪ *Hostilities between Israel and Syria erupt into the Six Day War.*

OCTOBER ▪ *Appointed by President Johnson, Thurgood Marshall becomes the first black United States Supreme Court Justice.*

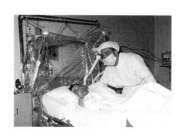

DECEMBER ▪ *Surgeon Christian Barnard performs the first heart transplant in Cape Town, South Africa.*

DECEMBER ▪ The Graduate, *directed by Mike Nichols and starring Dustin Hoffman and Ann Bancroft, is released to critical and popular acclaim.*

TECHNICAL DETAILS   **CAMERA** Rolleiflex
FILM Kodak 120 roll film
LENS 5 mm
SHUTTER & APERTURE 1/500th @ f8

Quiet Rain, Quiet Time

**BY TOSHIO SAKAI,
UNITED PRESS INTERNATIONAL**

When the monsoon rains sweep across Southeast Asia all other movement ceases. The downpour is sudden and heavy. Visibility is obscured. In cities vehicular traffic comes to a halt. Storm drains, dry moments before, become raging rivers. Even the war in Vietnam lets up, momentarily at least.

Toshio Sakai asked for a transfer to Vietnam after his Tokyo UPI colleague Kyoichi Sawada won a Pulitzer for photographs he had taken there in 1965. The wire service sent him and he had covered the war ever since—long enough to realize that the heavy rains would provide a quiet time and an opportunity for quiet pictures, which would stand in contrast to the usual fare in Vietnam.

GIs pulled on their ponchos against the downpour. One black GI stretched out atop the soggy sandbags of a bunker for a few moments of shut-eye. His mate, a white soldier, sat quietly in the background, rifle at the ready, on the lookout for the enemy. It was unlikely that an attack would come during the rainstorm. But because that is when attacks come, when they are least expected, the GIs took turns standing watch.

Sakai went about his photography. His sensitive insight into a quieter side of a violent war won the first Pulitzer Prize for feature photography.

Sakai would cover Vietnam until the end of the fighting. He would then work as a free-lancer before joining the French news agency, Agence France-Presse, and returned to news photography in the 1980s and 1990s.

TECHNICAL DETAILS	**CAMERA** Nikon
	FILM Kodak
	LENS 105 mm
	SHUTTER & APERTURE Unknown

1969 [NEWS]

Saigon Execution

BY EDDIE ADAMS, ASSOCIATED PRESS

On the eve of Tet, the Vietnamese lunar New Year in 1968, a massive Vietcong offensive struck with surprising strength and sharply increased the level of fighting all across Vietnam. The attackers moved into the cities, even into the courtyard of the U.S. Embassy in Saigon, where Vietcong troops blew a hole in the wall of the embassy building before being killed by marine guards and military policemen.

Americans at home, where the streets were increasingly the scene of antiwar demonstrations, wondered if the bloody, costly conflict would ever end. Eddie Adams, working his third stint in Vietnam for Associated Press, asked himself the same question on the second day of the offensive, February 1. He had covered the Korean War as a U.S. Marine photographer, and he had built a reputation as an excellent newspaper and AP photographer in the early 1960s. But on that day he was with National Broadcasting Company cameraman Vo Su. The two photographers, office neighbors who frequently shared transportation and news tips, had teamed up to investigate reports of fighting in Cholon, Saigon's Chinese section.

They looked around Cholon, but it appeared that fighting had eased up. A pagoda occupied by Vietcong had been recaptured by

JANUARY **1968** ■ *The North Vietnamese launch the Tet Offensive, a massive attack on enemy forces, breaking the lunar New Year truce.*

APRIL ■ *Martin Luther King Jr. is shot dead on the balcony of his Memphis, Tennessee hotel room. James Earl Ray is later tried and convicted of the crime.*

MAY ■ *Student riots in France force universities to close. Violent protests quickly spread to other industries and develop into a national crisis.*

Vietnamese marines and the debris from that battle littered the street, but not much more. They were about to depart when they heard shots a block or so away. Adams recalled that it sounded like infiltrators exchanging fire with Vietnamese army soldiers. The two moved toward the action.

Adams watched as two Vietnamese soldiers pulled a prisoner out of a doorway at the end of a street. The soldiers pushed and pulled what appeared to be a Vietcong infiltrator in a plaid shirt, his arms tied behind his back. They escorted the man toward the spot where Adams and Vo Su were located.

Eddie recalls that it looked like a typical New York City situation of policemen leading crime suspects before the press—called a "perp walk"—and he covered it that way. "I just followed the three of them as they walked toward us, making an occasional picture. When they were close—maybe five feet away—the soldiers stopped and backed away. I saw a man walk into my camera viewfinder from the left. He took a pistol out of his holster and raised it."

Even now, many years later, Adams pauses when he tells the story. He shakes his head in surprise, his eyes open a bit wider, and there is a slight shrug of astonishment. "I had no idea he would shoot. It was common to hold a pistol to the head of prisoners during questioning. So I prepared to make that picture— the threat, the interrogation. But that didn't happen. The man just pulled a pistol out of his holster, raised it to the VC's head and shot him in the temple. I made a picture at the same time."

The prisoner fell to the pavement, blood gushing from his head. Eddie made a shot or two of the man falling but then couldn't take any more and began to leave. The shooter, later identified as Lt. Col. Nguyen Loan, police chief of South Vietnam, walked up to Adams and said, "They killed many of my people, and yours, too."

TECHNICAL DETAILS   **CAMERA** Nikon
FILM Kodak
LENS 35 mm
SHUTTER & APERTURE 1/500th @ f 11

Adams comments, "And that's all he said. He just walked away."

Back in the office, Adams turned in his film and went to his hotel room, exhausted emotionally and upset by the incident. The pictures, the full sequence of the incident, were sent to the world by radiophoto.

The photograph was a sensation. It became a political statement and was printed and reprinted, appearing on placards at antiwar demonstrations. Antiwar advocates used it as an example of the

kind of allies the United States had in Vietnam. One writer described it as, "The shot not *heard* 'round the world, but *seen* 'round the world."

Loan was later promoted to Brigadier General, but the picture plagued him the remainder of his life. He and Adams, in fact, came to know each other later in the war, after Loan was wounded. Loan told Adams that his wife said he was foolish to not confiscate the film. But Loan never criticized Adams for the picture, saying that if he hadn't taken it, someone else would have. At war's end, Loan left Vietnam and took up residence in Virginia, where he ran a restaurant that eventually failed. Adams visited Loan at his business and, in the bathroom, saw inscribed on the wall, "We know who you are." Loan died of cancer in 1998.

Adams does not talk much about the picture, but he admits that it haunts him even now, decades later. "Two men died that day," he says, "the VC and Loan. Sometimes a picture can be misleading. Sometimes it does not tell the whole story. Many Vietnamese held great affection for Loan. He was not all that bad a guy. I don't say what he did was right, but he was fighting a war and he was up against some pretty bad people. Sometimes we tend to forget what the VC did to a lot of innocent citizens. I think of that sign in his restaurant, and I say to myself that I caused that sign to be there."

In addition to a Pulitzer, the photograph won a host of other awards. Adams appreciates the award, but he wishes he had won a Pulitzer for his other photography, for the more stylized, carefully made journalistic photography for which he was well known before he covered Vietnam.

In later years, Adams turned to freelance work, and produced photojournalistic stories and countless covers for magazines. He is the founder of The Eddie Adams Workshop, a four-day annual class for young photographers. At his farm in upstate New York, where the workshop is held, the group spends 30 minutes at a ceremony around a huge boulder, on which are inscribed the names of six photographers—close friends of Adams—killed in Vietnam. Wind whispers through a nearby stand of trees that were specially planted as a living monument to all the photographers who died covering the war. Like so many of the photographers and writers who covered Vietnam, Adams shares a special bond with those who survived as well as those who perished.

Adams's picture remains an icon, one of the century's most famous war photos; but it was not the last memorable picture from Vietnam. More would come as the conflict continued.

Guns on Campus

BY STEVE STARR, ASSOCIATED PRESS

In the late 1960s, activist students at colleges and universities across the nation adopted tactics such as campus demonstrations, sit-ins, riots, and office seizures to get their message across to the establishment. That message was that there was too much war, too much racism, too many poor, too close a tie between schools and government. To many Americans, it seemed like both the list of grievances and the conflict went on and on.

Steve Starr was the Associated Press photographer based in Albany, New York. Ithaca, the home of Cornell University, was his beat; so in April 1969, when he heard about trouble brewing there, Starr headed for the campus.

For some years, Cornell had actively recruited ghetto blacks, and it was close to setting up a black studies program. The university had established one dormitory exclusively for black women students. The black students wanted more, however. They sought amnesty for seven black students who had torn apart the administration building several months earlier, and they wanted the black studies program to be a separate college run by blacks. The Cornell president refused. Then a cross was burned in front of the black dorm.

Saturday, April 19, was the first day of Parent's Weekend. University President James A. Perkins had prepared a speech titled "The Stability of the University," but in the early morning hours, a group of black students took over the Student Union, rousting

TECHNICAL DETAILS   **CAMERA** Nikon
FILM Kodak
LENS 28 mm
SHUTTER & APERTURE Unknown shutter @ f2.8

FEBRUARY 1969 ■ *Palestinian terror groups unite under the umbrella of the Palestinian Liberation Organization, choosing Yasir Arafat as their leader.*

MARCH ■ *U.S. B-52 bombers secretly attack Communist bases in Cambodia.*

MARCH ■ *Golda Meir, formerly a schoolteacher in Wisconsin, is sworn in as Israel's fourth Premier.*

JULY ■ *The world holds its breath and the United States takes the lead in the space race as Neil Armstrong becomes the first man to step foot on the moon.*

parents staying there and sending them packing. The students intended to hold the building until their demands were met.

When Starr heard about the student takeover he headed for Ithaca. Once on the campus, he sized up the situation and concluded it would be an all-night event.

Starr recalled, "The next morning, rumors spread that the black students were armed. There were rumors about guns, but they were about armed whites taking over the Union. I thought I saw a guy in a window with what I thought looked like a gun, but before I could get my camera up he moved away." Starr knew that never before had students with guns taken over any U.S. campus, and if that were the case at Cornell, it would be an historic event.

After 34 hours, Perkins, who had long since cancelled his speech, granted amnesty to all the students involved in the incident. The university public relations staff, which up to that point had not released any useful information, told the media that the students would vacate the union momentarily. Starr moved to a position where he thought he would have a clear view of whatever might happen.

The door of the Student Union opened, and the black students walked out, armed to the teeth. Starr recalls, "There was a silence—a hushed silence. I felt a cold chill. The blacks came out with all these rifles, shotguns, knives, bandoliers."

As Starr shot his pictures, he knew he had historical material, but he was worried that students would start throwing rocks, or that the armed students would begin shooting. That didn't happen; the atmosphere remained tense, but there was no bloodshed.

The black students later said they had heard that other students on the campus were armed and that they feared for their lives. That was why they had smuggled the guns into the Union.

The Migrant's Stream

BY DALLAS KINNEY, THE *PALM BEACH (FLORIDA) POST*

Migrant workers start in the south in January each year and, with the predictability of the seasons, follow the ripening crops north. First they pick and load fruit in Florida, then move on to the truck farms of the mid-Atlantic states. By the time they reach New Jersey, the vegetables there are ready for harvest, and that work is followed by harvesting in New England. This annual trek of backbreaking labor delivers a bountiful harvest to the dinner tables of America.

In the late 1960s, the workers—most of them African-Americans who knew no life but to toil in the fields—fared poorly. They were victims of a complex agrarian society that put them at the bottom of a hierarchy and paid them only a few dollars a day for hours of stoop labor.

Dallas Kinney, a *Palm Beach Post* photographer, thought that his paper should tell the story of the Palm Beach County migrant workers forthrightly, strongly, and in graphic detail, but he knew he would have to convince his editors

"I was an Iowa farm boy," Kinney recalls, "and I knew what harvest labor was like. The migrants were at it all the time as

TECHNICAL DETAILS   **CAMERA** Leica and Nikon
FILM Kodak
LENS Various, from 20 mm to 200 mm
SHUTTER & APERTURE Various

JULY **1969** ■ *Mary Jo Kopechne is killed when the car she's a passenger in, driven by Senator Edward Kennedy, crashes off of a bridge into water.*

AUGUST ■ *Woodstock Music & Art Fair brings together 300,000 people, epitomizing the spirit of love and sharing for which the era would become famous.*

AUGUST ■ *Actress Sharon Tate and four others are murdered in her Los Angeles home. Charles Manson is convicted of the crime.*

SEPTEMBER ■ *After 15 years as president, North Vietnamese leader Ho Chi Minh dies at age 79.*

they followed the harvest stream northward. They were poorly paid, ill with serious diseases that were crippling, and with little education for the kids who moved constantly with the family. And they were seldom seen, kind of hidden in the back roads of the countryside."

Kinney and the reporter who would write the story told their editors that they would take them to lunch to explain their proposal. Lunch turned out to be a sandwich at a migrant labor camp, where Kinney showed the editors how the migrants lived in tar-paper shacks and how kids played in the dusty lanes between hovels.

"They got the point," Kinney says, and the paper backed the story to the hilt.

The first pictures were shot in color, and it was expected that the pictures would be printed that way; but Kinney decided to throw away his early days of work. "Color," he said, "made it look too pretty. I switched to black and white and started over."

Kinney printed the first set of pictures and pasted them up in the editor's office one evening. The next morning, when Kinney's editor walked into the room, he was more convinced than ever that the pictures should be displayed dramatically in the paper.

The *Post* published a series of stories, each of which was introduced with a large picture on the front page followed by more pictures and text inside. The *Post's* affluent Palm Beach readership clearly and dramatically saw a side of the community that was seldom, if ever, presented so forcefully.

Kinney's picture series was the first of its kind in Pulitzer history. It represented an approach to photojournalism in which the photographer sought out a continuing story and documented it through an expansive presentation over several days. That a photographer such as Kinney would envision that kind of project was perhaps a natural reaction to the establishment of a Pulitzer feature photography award in 1968. Other stories using this approach would win Pulitzers in future years.

Death on the Campus

BY JOHN FILO, FREELANCE

It is difficult to say what began the inevitable movement toward death on Ohio's Kent State University campus on May 4, 1970; but the events of that day, and a single photograph documenting them, had a lasting impact on the nation. The declaration by President Nixon on April 30 that U.S. forces would enter Cambodia to deny sanctuary to those who attacked American troops led to violent student demonstrations that closed 75 universities before the end of the academic year. At Kent State that weekend, police had used tear gas to disperse rowdy students after a beer bust in a downtown bar, and demonstrations at the campus ROTC building had ended with the building ablaze, firemen attacked with rocks, and the National Guard called in. Guardsmen in helmets and black gas masks battled with students on Sunday night, arresting 150.

When the bell in the university tower rang at midday on Monday, May 4, twenty-one-year-old journalist student John Filo, who was working as a photo-lab tech in Taylor Hall, the journalism building, grabbed a camera and film and left the building to photograph a student rally that had been planned for noon.

What Filo found on the lush, green, leafy campus was a gathering of a thousand protesting students, a rally the National Guard attempted to disperse. As Filo came upon the scene, the guardsmen had formed two skirmish lines; the students were throwing rocks, and the guardsmen were returning fire with tear gas. Filo photographed both sides of the confrontation, moving from students to guardsmen. One group of soldiers started to back up a hill, and the students advanced toward them. Their rocks fell short, but the students were moving closer.

At the crest of the hill, Filo recalls, the troops stopped, dropped to one knee, and opened fire. Filo was sure the shots were blanks, fired to intimidate the students; but then, in his viewfinder, he saw a bullet hit a metal sculpture, pass through it, and smack into a tree. Several students fell before the gunfire, dead or wounded; others dove to the ground to avoid danger. Filo realized that the troops had fired live ammunition, and that he was the only one standing up and photographing the scene. He later wondered how he had escaped injury when so many others were wounded.

When the shooting stopped, Filo decided to move out of the area; but as he turned to depart, he saw the body of Jeffrey Miller some few feet away. Miller had been hit in the neck, and in just a few moments, a large pool of blood formed. A young girl ran toward the body.

Filo recalls, "The girl came up and knelt over the body and let out a God-awful scream. That made me hit the shutter button—it was instinct, a reflex action. Just one frame." Only three frames remained on his roll, but he knew he had a picture that documented the terrible events at Kent State.

His memory of the remainder of the day is that of the fear he felt—fear that the film would somehow be taken from him, that he

had missed the picture, that a coverup would emerge and his picture would be involved. He made his way to the *Valley Daily News*, a newspaper in Tarentum, Pennsylvania, where he worked as an intern. From there the picture was transmitted to the world via Associated Press.

Initially, some people disbelieved the picture, convinced that it was somehow faked. These critics asked about the girl being in just the right spot, about the way the student's body lay on the sidewalk, about the way the blood flowed in a straight, even path away from the body. The caption originally given to the picture read, "Coed Screams," but it turned out that the girl was a fourteen-year-old Florida runaway who was on the campus because she was curious. The unfortunate use of the word *coed* encouraged critics to attack the picture's credibility.

Nevertheless, the photo quickly became an icon, that special kind of picture that somehow sums up a greater series of events. The criticism of the picture's credibility was soon brushed aside as the death toll—four students dead and five seriously wounded—became known. Filo's picture joined the collection of photographic icons that forever would be part of the history of the Vietnam War,

TECHNICAL DETAILS   **CAMERA** Nikormat
                          FILM Kodak
                          LENSES Zoom lens, 43 mm to 86 mm
                          SHUTTER & APERTURE Unknown

that are symbolic of the war fought on American streets as well as that in the Asian countryside.

Filo was presented the news photography Pulitzer Prize for 1971, and he later joined Associated Press. He also worked for the *Philadelphia Inquirer, Newsweek,* the *Camden (New Jersey) Courier* and on the photo staff of CBS television.

The girl, Mary Ann Vecchio, was reunited with her parents because of the picture, but she has said that the photo brought her publicity she did not want. It astounded her that critics of the student demonstrations reviled her because she appeared in the photo. She eventually settled in Las Vegas and married. She and Filo did not see each other until 25 years later, when they met once again at an educational conference in Boston.

1971 [FEATURE]

A Warehouse for People

BY JACK DYKINGA, THE *CHICAGO SUN-TIMES*

Jack Dykinga received one of the earliest of the Pulitzer Prizes to be awarded for images that documented a social issue, as opposed to a news event. The photos he took at the Lincoln and Dixon State Schools for the mentally retarded near Chicago were at once artistic and terrifying, and they shocked Chicagoans.

Dykinga's purpose in visiting the schools—which he called warehouses for unfortunates—was to highlight the effect a proposed reduction of state funding would have on what little care these institutions provided.

The impact of the scenes he encountered was so strong that Dykinga was unable to use his camera during the first hours of his visit to the so-called "cottages," which were actually more like hospital wards.

"I just watched. I was overwhelmed by the horror of it," he said later.

His report described overwhelming odors, retarded children and adults smeared with feces, and beds wet from urine. He talked of severely overworked staff members; the four aides, for example,

who attended a hundred patients were forced to feed the retarded much too quickly just in order to get around to them all.

Dykinga brought to the assignment a fine eye for composition and detail and a graphic simplicity that enhanced the drama of the photos and the story. The result of the photos' publication in the *Sun-Times* was that funding was extended at its then-current rate. More importantly, Dykinga's pictures sensitized legislators to the desperate, loveless existence the mentally handicapped endured in the schools.

After he won the Pulitzer, Dykinga moved to the Southwest and turned his pictorialist's eye on the environment. He quickly established himself as one of the nation's most prominent landscape photographers, coupling his photographer's eye with the journalist's perspective of environmental reporting. He lectured widely and produced several books; one entitled *Stone Canyon* was influential in the federal government's decision to make the area he photographed a national monument.

NOVEMBER 1970 ■ *Chilean president Salvador Allende Gossens is the first Marxist to be elected head of a government in the Western Hemisphere by a democratic majority.*

NOVEMBER ■ *Charles de Gaulle, the controversial French leader who represented France like no other, dies.*

DECEMBER ■ *The north tower of the World Trade Center is topped out, making it the world's tallest building at 1,350 feet.*

TECHNICAL DETAILS   **CAMERA** Leica and Nikon
FILM Kodak
LENS Various
SHUTTER & APERTURE Various

Revenge At The Racetrack

BY HORST FAAS AND MICHEL LAURENT, ASSOCIATED PRESS

December evenings, cooled and refreshed by breezes that temper the day's sun, are pleasant on the Indian subcontinent, but on the night of December 18, 1971, Horst Faas and his Associated Press colleague Michel Laurent were far from comfortable. The two men, veterans of many years covering Vietnam, were not strangers to violence and death, but the night of revenge they photographed at the racetrack in Dacca, Bangladesh had shaken them as much as anything Vietnam's fury had ever offered.

The history that leads to that night is confusing, blurred by the cultural, historical, and political fabric woven tightly across the region. The end of British colonial rule in India in 1947 left behind a strange geography. India was created as a state, as was Pakistan; but Pakistan was separated into eastern and western sections, with a thousand-mile stretch of India separating them. Over the next several decades, major tensions grew between the two Pakistani regions. By March 1971, a secessionist group in East Pakistan wanted to call itself Bangladesh, declared independence, and was willing to go to war to make it so.

Faas and Laurent, based in Vietnam, were assigned to cover the story. Faas worked out of Calcutta, India; Laurent worked out of Dacca.

To prevent the announced secession, the federal government, based in West Pakistan, unleashed a reign of butchery in the

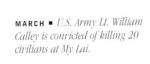

JANUARY 1971 ■ *All in the Family debuts, defying longstanding taboos against ethnic and bathroom humor on television.*

MARCH ■ *U.S. Army Lt. William Calley is convicted of killing 20 civilians at My Lai.*

APRIL ■ *Igor Stravinsky, one of the century's greatest composers, dies at 88.*

JUNE ■ *U.S. Supreme Court overturns attempts to stop* The New York Times *and* Washington Post *from publishing the* Pentagon Papers.

On December 18, an event billed as a rally to mark the beginning of the new nation was to be held at the Dacca Racetrack. When Faas arrived in Dacca that day, he could not locate Laurent, who was out photographing. Faas walked around the city looking for picture possibilities and visited the university. He recalls, "It was a bloody day, with random gangs killing a person here or there. There were many beatings."

In the afternoon, he decided to head for the Dacca Racetrack, where he found Laurent. A dais had been setup, and speakers sang

newly named Bangladesh and followed with military encounters that defeated the eastern forces. The violence was so severe that ten million refugees fled into India, leaving behind some one million slain. Victory for West Pakistan was short-lived, however, when India backed the eastern guerrilla movement known as Mukti Bahini. As the Indian troops drove toward Dacca, Horst Faas with them, stories emerged about the executions, torture, and brutality West Pakistanis had directed against the easterners, with the Pakistani military for the most part looking the other way. On December 17, the western side surrendered to the combined forces of the Indian army and the local guerrillas, and the new nation of Bangladesh was thereby ensured. There remained a bitter taste in Bangladesh over the recent merciless slaughter, however.

the praises of the new order. Faas and Laurent took pictures, sometimes of the crowd, sometimes of the new political leaders. They worked together, at times they separated.

Faas saw a large crowd of several thousand spectators standing by as Mukti Bahini guerrillas pushed four bound captives off the back of a truck into a cleared area. These prisoners were known as *razakars,* a kind of local militia that worked under the command of the West Pakistan government. They were accused of rape and murder.

Laurent joined Faas at the scene as the Bahinis tortured the bound prisoners by burning them with cigarettes. Faas twice asked them to stop, then he and Laurent moved away because they thought the event was being staged for the camera and hoped their departure would end the public brutality. No one noticed their leaving, however, and the torture continued. Faas and Laurent moved back, but stayed in the crowd and watched.

One of the political leaders stepped down from the dais and picked up a weapon with mounted bayonet. Faas and Laurent sensed something was about to happen, and they moved to the front of the crowd. The man with the bayonet calmly, carefully, and deliberately pushed the bayonet into one of the bound prisoners with an action that was meant to wound, not to kill. He then passed his weapon to a guerilla fighter, and the Bahinis used their weapons on all the prisoners—stabbing at them and plunging the bayonets into their bodies. Faas and Laurent maneuvered themselves back into the circle of spectators.

Faas recalls, "During the terrible torture, sweat ran down my face and my hands were trembling so much I couldn't change the film. When the bayoneting started, Michel was just as pale as the victims. It went on and on. The crowd cheered and took no notice of us. I hoped the men would die quickly, but it took almost an hour. Then the mob came in to finish the execution with their trampling feet. I hope and pray that no AP man has to see such horror again."

Suddenly members of the mob asked the two photographers what they were doing, so Faas and Laurent moved away. A couple of spectators chased them, but the effort was half-hearted. The two photographers dumped their film into a single bag and worked their way out of the area, fearful that their cameras would attract the attention of the executioners. They might be the next target of the already aroused crowd.

At 4 a.m., Faas used his Indian army accreditation to return to Calcutta, where he processed the film and took prints to the Indian communications center for transmission to London. Indian authorities in control of the communications facilities released some of the images—mostly the torture pictures—but they refused to permit transmission of the bayoneting pictures. The result was that the story was played out in the worldwide media for a much longer

TECHNICAL DETAILS   **CAMERA** Leica
FILM Kodak
LENS Various, range from 21 mm
to 200 mm
SHUTTER & APERTURE Various

period than it might have been. The written story was published first, and the pictures that were transmitted were printed a day later. Faas and Laurent sent their film and the censored photos to London by courier and the bayoneting pictures were ultimately transmitted to the world from there.

Although there was some criticism of the two photographers by people who felt their presence had encouraged the action, others said that the pictures generated international pressures that improved the treatment of the ethnic minority in Bangladesh.

Faas and Laurent returned to their duties in Vietnam. Faas soon left Asia for an AP assignment in London. Laurent was killed in Cambodia some three years later during the final stages of the Vietnamese war.

When the Pulitzer Prize for the Dacca racetrack photo was awarded to the two men, Faas became the first photographer to be honored with a second award. He had won for his Vietnam coverage in 1965.

1976 [FEATURE]

Cameras On Busing

BY THE STAFF OF THE LOUISVILLE (KENTUCKY) *COURIER-JOURNAL*

The question for the staff of the *Louisville (Kentucky) Courier-Journal* was not whether there would be busing—the federal courts had mandated that—but how would it be covered by the paper's photographers and reporters.

Tom Hardin, then director of photography for a staff of 27, recalled that the simple goal the staff sought was to keep everything in balance—to keep the pictures' subject matter in balance, to avoid pictures of subjects who were performing for the media, to tell both sides of the story without fear or favor. These guidelines meant that if there were two people protesting, a photo should show the protest as a two-person gathering; if there are a thousand gathered, the picture should show that. As it turned out, both scenarios materialized.

Obtaining balance and perspective would not be as easy as it sounded. Feelings ran high on the issue, not only in Louisville but around the country; and many believed there was no option for achieving equal education for children except to bus them. An equally large and vocal group believed that busing was plain wrong.

Busing was to begin on the first day of school, September 4, 1975. In one sense, Louisville lucked out during the early days because a school boycott reduced the number of children that actually moved about the city from 130,000 to the 90,000. Nearly 600 yellow school buses ferried these children to their classrooms. In some cases, whole student bodies were switched in an effort to meet the federal government's mandate.

The *Courier-Journal*'s coverage continued for months, as photographers chronicled the preparations, the actual busing, and the many weeks of controversy and activity that swirled around the issue.

"The signature picture," Hardin says, "was a wonderful shot of a black child and a white child shaking hands in an otherwise empty classroom." Other key pictures included one of a police officer seated squarely in the middle of a bus as it lumbered on its way to school and others that depicted large crowds in support of, or opposed to, the busing.

The picture portfolio presented to the Pulitzer committee consisted of 70 photos that portrayed much of what happened in Louisville related to the busing issue that year. Still others were shots of fighting and peaceful protests, of kids together, and of police watching over the activities of both the Ku Klux Klan and those who supported busing.

All in all, the *Courier-Journal* presented a balanced picture report of a troubled time in its history, a report that did not incite, and was not sensational; it presented in the proper perspective a story that affected nearly every Louisville family.

JULY 1975 ■ *Arthur Ashe beats Jimmy Connors at Wimbledon.*

JULY ■ *Chinese archeologists discover 6,000 funerary figures dating from 221-206 B.C.*

OCTOBER ■ *New York City faces a grave financial crisis; President Ford refuses to help.*

NOVEMBER ■ *Generalissimo Francisco Franco, who ruled Spain for 36 years, dies.*

TECHNICAL DETAILS   **CAMERA** Nikon and Leica
FILM Kodak
LENS Various
SHUTTER & APERTURE Various

The Flag in the Plaza

BY STANLEY FORMAN, THE BOSTON HERALD-AMERICAN

Boston Herald-American staff photographer Stanley Forman always listened to the police scanner in his car when he cruised the city's streets. The previous year, a scanner message had alerted him to a fire, and the pictures he made from it won a Pulitzer Prize. Although that was not likely to happen again, it did not reduce the value of the police radio as the source of tips for many of the paper's daily stories. The sooner a photographer was on the scene of a possible story, the greater the chance for telling photos.

On May 4, 1976, Forman heard the police dispatcher report trouble in City Hall Plaza, and he turned in that direction.

Like many cities in the United States in that bicentennial year, South Boston was in the throes of a school busing issue. Busing too often brought out the worst in people, and Boston was no exception. Plans were underway to transport schoolchildren from one section of the city to another with the goal of improving educational levels of the city's underprivileged.

The police dispatcher's call was prompted by students who marched in City Hall Plaza and chanted antibusing slogans. They were there, they said, to make demands on the council; but when they arrived, the city chambers were closed. They milled about, riled and angry.

Unaware of what was happening, black attorney Theodore Landsmark walked into the scene, headed for offices in City Hall. A group of some two dozen students spotted him; and in a sudden burst of racial hatred, they attacked him.

Forman arrived moments ahead of the police, just as the melee started, and he began taking pictures.

"They were all over him," he recalls. "They were punching him, hitting him, and they knocked him to the ground. In my viewfinder, I saw one student carrying a long flagpole with a good-sized flag mounted on it. Some students held the helpless man steady as a target, and the student with the pole struck him repeatedly in the head with the end of the pole."

The police arrived, broke up the attack and rushed Landsmark to a hospital, where he was treated for a broken nose and facial cuts. Much of his body was covered in bruises.

The *Herald-American* published Forman's graphic picture in a large size. It was widely distributed, and it became one of the year's most ironic photos—a flagpole carrying America's patriotic symbol, the Stars and Stripes, had been used as a weapon for an unjust cause inspired by racial hatred. In terms of the Pulitzer Prize, of course, the irony does not end there. The picture was only the second award-winning photo in which an American flag played such a significant role; the first was the raising of Old Glory on Iwo Jima.

Forman was the first photographer to win a Pulitzer Prize in two consecutive years.

TECHNICAL DETAILS   **CAMERA** Nikon
FILM Kodak
LENS 20 mm
SHUTTER & APERTURE Unknown

A Face in the Crowd

BY ROBIN HOOD, THE CHATTANOOGA (TENNESSEE) *NEWS FREE PRESS*

The Vietnam War was past but its memory lingered on, refreshed constantly in the minds of those who fought there by the common incidents of everyday life. In Chattanooga, for example, as in many American towns and cities, Armed Forces Day inspired a parade that honored veterans, including Vietnam veterans.

Photographer Robin Hood of the *News Free Press*, himself a Vietnam veteran, walked the parade route, camera in hand, in search of a good picture. It was in Vietnam, in fact, that Hood learned his trade. He started out as a public information officer guiding the press through the military maze to get their stories. Then he picked up a camera and, with coaching by military photographers, learned to take pictures. *The News Free Press* hired him when he returned home.

Now it was 1976, only a year after the war shutdown, and the memory of many still carried the images of harried helicopters taking off from the roof of the U.S. embassy. Here on the parade route Hood caught sight of a Vietnamese refugee family waving the flags of their newfound homeland as they watched a parade that must have been hard for them to understand. He took pictures of the family.

Hood continued on along the parade route trying keep his camera dry in the chilly rain of a bleak day. He photographed young veterans and old timers out to catch a little nostalgia.

Then he saw the man, legs lost on an Asian battlefield, wearing a military poncho and an army shirt against the rain, his child nestled in his lap between the wheels of the chair that carried him The man watched the Vietnamese wave their flags.

The circle was complete: Vietnamese family in a new land and a warrior who fought for them but would carry his wound forever. Hood took a picture of the man. It showed him proud and strong, somehow symbolic of all that had gone before but with the determination to move forward.

The man's name was Eddie Robinson. To Hood, Robinson was the star of the parade that rainy day, a veteran who had given much so that others could live free.

Hood continued as a photographer at the paper but eventually opened his own publishing business.

TECHNICAL DETAILS

CAMERA Nikon
FILM Kodak
LENS 105 mm
SHUTTER & APERTURE Unknown

AUGUST 1976 ■ *West Point accepts women cadets for the first time.*

SEPTEMBER ■ *China's Mao Tse-tung dies of Parkinson's disease at age 82.*

NOVEMBER ■ *Democrat Jimmy Carter wins the U.S. presidential election.*

DECEMBER ■ *Sylvester Stallone stars in* Rocky.

A Time In The Spotlight

BY JOHN BLAIR, FREELANCE FOR UNITED PRESS INTERNATIONAL

Anthony Kiritsis planned it carefully. First, the shotgun: .12 gauge, sawed-off. Second, the wire: reliable but flexible. The arrangement: he figured out exactly how to wire the weapon. The timing: he would wait for the man to arrive at work.

It was Tuesday, February 8, 1977, when the plan went into action. Richard Hall, president of the Meridian Mortgage Company, entered his Indianapolis office at his usual early-morning hour. Kiritsis had been waiting for him; he yanked out his shotgun as Hall entered and quickly wired the shotgun to Hall's neck and head. He then wired the weapon to himself and to the trigger of the shotgun.

The plan had worked fine so far; Kiritsis had Hall where he wanted him. The two men were attached as one, with the shotgun in the middle. If Hall tried to escape, the shotgun would fire into his head. If police snipers shot Kiritsis, he would fall and his weight would pull the trigger. Either way, Hall was a goner.

Kiritsis was in control at last, unlike his position of previous months. Hall's company had loaned Kiritsis money which, combined with his life's savings, he had invested in the construction of a mall. Kiritsis felt Hall had refused to back him in the business, even encouraging others to avoid investment in the mall so that Meridian could foreclose.

Kiritsis, Hall, and the shotgun took to the street, where a passing police car stopped to investigate. Kiritsis forced the officer to drive him and Hall to Kiritsis's apartment, and a classic standoff was underway.

On Wednesday afternoon, freelance photographer John Blair joined the United Press International staff to help with the coverage of the story. By that time, hundreds of police, including a SWAT team, were on the scene, as were news media, in great numbers. It looked as though the standoff would last a long time, so UPI rented an apartment nearby and set up a portable picture operation.

Events of this kind can capture the attention of the world, and that is just what John Kiritsis had done. He was perceived, rightly or wrongly, as the poor little guy who had been done in by powerful business interests that rolled over him, his modest fortune, his very life.

By the third day of the story, the authorities and Kiritsis had negotiated a solution to the encounter. Kiritsis would get immunity from the local prosecutor's office and be given an opportunity to describe his grievances to the world via a press conference.

Blair was in the lobby of the apartment house as Kiritsis, Hall, and the ever-present shotgun, still wired in place, stepped into the media setup. It was the first time most people had seen the two men. Blair found himself standing so close to the scene that, as he looked at Hall, Kiritsis, and the muzzle of the shot-

JANUARY 1977 ■ *The television mini-series* Roots *is aired for an unprecedented eight nights in a row, breaking all previous viewership records.*

MAY ■ *George Lucas's film* Star Wars *is released.*

JULY ■ *The 799-mile Trans-Alaskan oil pipeline begins full operations.*

gun, he could have reached out and touched the weapon, had he wanted to. Fearful there would be shooting, Blair stepped off to the side.

He recalled, "Kiritsis shouted right at me, 'get those god-damned television cameras rolling.'"

And then Kiritsis followed with a rambling presentation of his grievances. He wept openly at the injustice done to him. Hall was bleary-eyed; and when Kiritsis demanded that Hall forgive the $130,000 loan and apologize, Hall was unable to respond articulately, no doubt exhausted by the days of captivity and the ever-present gun at the back of his head.

Kiritsis rambled on, wild-eyed; he waved his arm, pointed dramatically at the disoriented Hall, and told the world that he was a national hero. But the perception of the little guy versus the big guy dissipated. Kiritsis was obviously out of control.

Near the end of Kiritsis's ranting, Blair took his dramatic Pulitzer-winning picture of the confrontation.

The press conference over, the cops cleared the lobby. Kiritsis gathered himself and walked Hall into a nearby apartment. Blair remembers the deathly silence that gripped the crowd outside the building, a silence shattered by the unmistakable roar of a shotgun. Everyone wondered who was dead, who was alive.

Kiritsis walked out unarmed and surrendered to the police. Hall was alive in the apartment. Kiritsis had released him and fired the shotgun into the air from the apartment patio. It was his final gesture of defiance and protest.

Hall was taken to a hospital for rest and observation. Kiritsis later was tried and found innocent by reason of insanity, then confined to a mental institution.

TECHNICAL DETAILS **CAMERA** Pentax
FILM Kodak
LENS 20 mm
SHUTTER & APERTURE Unknown

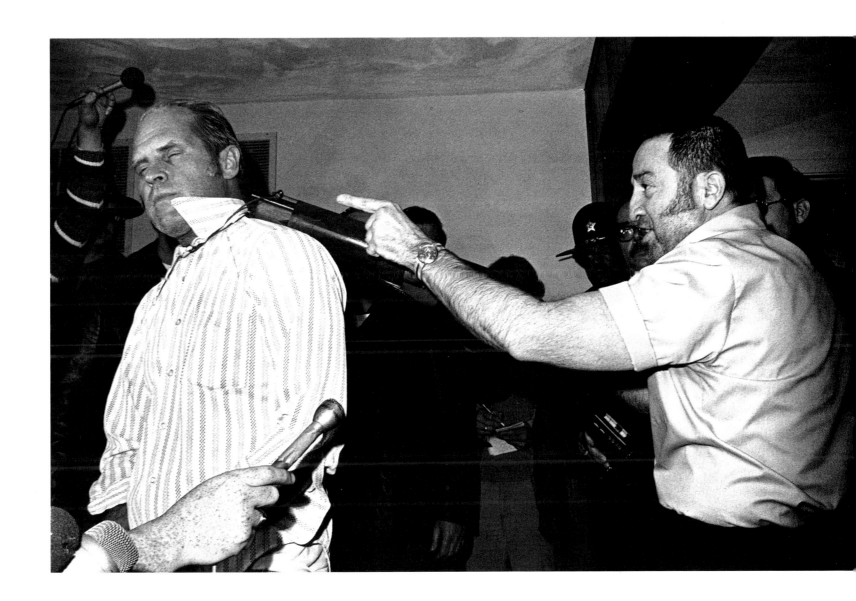

Boston Snowbound

BY THE STAFF OF THE *BOSTON HERALD*

Kevin Cole, chief photographer of *The Boston Herald*, stood waist deep in water as he photographed, on his day off, a raging ocean surf near his home in Plymouth, Massachusetts, that chopped away the shoreline and carried chunks of earth into the sea. A wind had suddenly whipped up, and that's what enticed Cole, who had lived next to the water most of his life, to the seashore to photograph. The water was not particularly cold, despite being early February, but it suddenly chilled sharply and Cole knew that Boston was in for trouble. As it turned out, the storm of February 8, 1978, caused the worst winter trouble in some 200 years.

The storm started quietly, with just a light snowfall. Forecasters had predicted a few inches, not considered much to hardy New Englanders who dealt regularly with northeasters and other furies of an unpredictable Mother Nature.

As the snow continued to fall, forecasts were altered. In Boston, the steady snowfall emptied offices early, and children were dismissed from school early in an effort to get them home before snow clogged the highways.

Snowplows swung into action, likewise hoping to get ahead of what by then had been forecast as a powerful storm. The snow fell and fell, into the evening, all night, into the morning.

Cole recalls that, when he woke up on Tuesday, he could not see out the windows of his house, which was buried in snow.

NOVEMBER 1978 ■ *Led by cult leader Reverend Jim Jones, over 900 people commit mass suicide at the Jonestown, Guyana, compound of the Peoples Temple.*

DECEMBER ■ *Karl Wallenda, patriarch of the famous aerialist troup, falls to his death in Puerto Rico.*

DECEMBER ■ *Menachem Begin and Anwar el-Sadat win the Nobel Peace Prize.*

Boston highways were closed down. Route 128, the major highway that encircled the city, was clogged by a mass of some 3,000 cars that had been caught and stranded by the snowfall. The wind remained despite a clearing, even brightly sunny day.

Cole knew Boston was out of business so he headed southeast from Plymouth, toward Hyannis, on Cape Cod. It was possible, he thought, to charter a plane in Hyannis and fly back to Boston with the film he made the previous day and any pictures he might take during his return to the city. He drove along a highway with a single lane of traffic opened; the two sides of the road were high walls of snow. "It was like riding a toboggan," Cole says. "All you could see was what was in front of you."

Once at the Hyannis airport, Cole went to the Discover Flying School, where a pilot said he'd take him to Boston if he could get into the air despite the winds. He took Cole to his plane, which turned out to be a small, two-seater aircraft used primarily for local flights. Cole recalls, "I wondered where the rubber bands were to wind it up."

The plane took off, however, and Cole saw for the first time the extensive shoreline destruction caused by the storm. Houses were tumbled about like toy blocks; some were actually in the sea, pulled out by the tides and winds. Seawalls of concrete and steel were twisted and washed away. People were atop their homes,

TECHNICAL DETAILS **CAMERA** Nikon
FILM Kodak
LENS Various
SHUTTER & APERTURE Various

desperately awaiting rescue. Waves driven by gale force winds continued to pound the shoreline and flood the coastal towns. Being in the small plane gave Cole a unique perspective from which to photograph the storm's damage.

Cole saw Minot Light, a lighthouse and popular historical landmark, in the distance. Giant waves crashed against it, and he wanted to get a picture. They flew out to the lighthouse, and as the plane circled several times to get in position for a picture Cole became airsick. As they turned away to head back, Cole made one final shot of the lighthouse engulfed in the white, churning water of a huge wave that crashed over the structure.

Other *Herald* staffers had their own adventures documenting the storm. Paul Benoit, for example, walked ten miles through the snow-covered landscape to Revere to photograph the rescue of some 1,000 people from that isolated coastal town.

Power was lost throughout the area, and back at the paper staffers camped out on cots and desks, trying their best to get ready to go to press. Cole made it back, as did Benoit, and their pictures, along with those of the few others from the staff who were able to make it to the *Herald* office, were featured in a special tabloid picture section added to the regular broadsheet edition. The portfolio won the Pulitzer Prize for the *Herald*'s photo staff as a group.

tugging at the reins of their horses as well as handling the controls of a small helicopter. In each case there was but one goal in mind, to drive cattle.

While the helicopters and pickup trucks were part of the cowboy scene, Hagler's pictures from many weeks on the range told a story of men who lived and worked the way they had for more than a century—close to the earth and hardened by the sun, the wind, and the dust of the trail.

"The toughest part of the coverage was the boredom, the waiting for something to happen. But you know, you get to know the people; and pretty soon you are invisible, and that's when pictures happen."

Hagler insisted on doing the story in black and white. "It's gritty," he said, "like the dust on the prairie. Black and white is somehow dirtier and fit this story better than color. I didn't want these guys to look like the Marlboro Man, because that was not what they were."

The product of Hagler's determination and his hours on the prairie was a series of classic photos that could have been made by photographers who roamed the west more than a century ago to record America's western expansion with huge cameras, glass plates, and wet-film processes. Hagler's pictures, made at a time when astronauts walked on the moon and nuclear submarines glided beneath the polar extremities of the earth, showed modern cowboys to be the same rugged individuals of yesteryear whose lifestyle had changed little from that of their predecessors.

The paper's Sunday magazine published 40 pictures of cowboys one weekend, and then a second story the following Sunday on just one individual said to be the oldest cowboy working.

"You know," Hagler muses 20 years later during a quick break from his freelancing work in Dallas, "people still recall those pictures. When I introduce myself as Skeeter Hagler they frequently say, 'Didn't you make some pictures about cowboys.' That makes me feel good."

TECHNICAL DETAILS   **CAMERA** Nikon
FILM Kodak black & white and
Kodachrome
LENS Various, ranging from 35 mm to
600 mm
SHUTTER & APERTURE Various

Color and Digital Photography, Women Photographers, and the Africa Pulitzers

The Pulitzer Prize winners in the final two decades of the 20th century reflected the dynamic nature of the era. Color pictures dominated the awards, but pictures from Africa also appeared for the first time, photographs by women were submitted in greater numbers, and the influence of new technology was apparent.

The most notable change in Pulitzer Prize photography was the ascendancy of, and ultimately the predominance of, color pictures. This was made possible by advances in newspaper technology—particularly in the area of digital picture scanning and transmission—that opened the door to faster, easier, and more economical reproduction of color.

In the late 1970s and the early 1980s, the only newspapers that used color widely were the handful that had taken a leadership role in its development. In the latter part of the 1980s and the early 1990s, the Associated Press abandoned the antique technologies of picture transmission that had existed unchanged for generations and switched to high-speed digital transmission. This technology not only delivered high-quality pictures from all corners of the globe, it also made handling color photographs easier and more efficient. The equipment used for wire pictures also accommodated local pictures, so news photographers soon could venture into an all-color world.

The emergence of color in newspapers was mirrored in the Pulitzer Prizes. In the century's final decade, only three of the 20 awards were for black-and-white photography.

In past years, editors had debated the "reality" of color, asking whether color pictures were as truthful as black and white. It wasn't truth—or the lack of it—that actually hampered the use of color, however; it was the poor quality of newspaper color reproduction which readers found confusing. With reproduction technology under control, newspapers were able to print color photography that rivaled that of magazines. And readers loved it.

Prior to the 1970s, relatively few women chose photojournalism as a career. Their numbers increased in the post-Vietnam war years, and that change was reflected in the increasing number of women photographers who won Pulitzer Prizes. Except for the amateur Virginia Schau, who captured the 1954 Pulitzer with her Box Brownie picture of a truck dangling from a bridge (page 39), there were no women Pulitzer-winning photographers until 1986, when Carol Guzy and Michel duCille won for their photographs of the devastating impact of a volcanic eruption in Colombia (pages 174-177). Guzy would win another Pulitzer in 1995 for her work in Haiti (page 227). In the 1990s, three women captured Pulitzers, and there were women on Associated Press photographic teams that won awards covering the Olympics, politics, and international affairs.

These women did not necessarily bring a different perspective to news photography. Based on the pictures they made and the subject matter they covered, they clearly were professional journalists producing pictures of the same high quality as their male counterparts. Women won Pulitzers for hometown spot news (Annie Wells in 1997 for a gripping picture of a river rescue), for difficult foreign assignments (Guzy in Haiti in 1995 and Martha Rial in Africa in 1998); and for challenging subject matter (Stephanie Welsh in 1996 for her picture story on female genital mutilation in Africa).

As news photographers pursued stories in critical hotspots around the globe, it was only natural that new datelines from different countries enter the Pulitzer chronology. In 1978, J. Ross Baughman's pictures from Rhodesia won the first Pulitzer from an African location. In the next two decades 11 more Pulitzers, out of some 40 that were presented, were for pictures made in Africa. The pictures honored were in classic Pulitzer tradition; some were picture series and others were single pictures, but all were unrelenting images from a continent that was struggling with the horror of genocide, hunger, and revolution.

The period's final hallmark—digital cameras and portable satellite telephones—came in the late 1990s. To understand the impact of this new technology, one has to go back to Max Desfor, who was the Pulitzer winner in 1951 for his pictures from the Korean War. Desfor used a cumbersome 4x5 Speed Graphic and made his pictures on 4x5 film carried in a film pack. He shipped his film via courier to an air base in Japan, where it was picked up by AP Tokyo staff and processed; a few selected pictures were transmitted to San Francisco or New York on unreliable radiophoto circuits. Sometimes pictures had to be transmitted repeatedly before they actually were received at their destination. Frequently, otherwise worthwhile pictures were not published because the quality of radio transmission was so poor. Color was out of the question. The field situation was not all that different in the Vietnam years.

By the late 1990s, photographers, especially wire-service photographers, could use digital cameras in which electronic chips replaced film. Technicians saw images on computer screens, not as prints in the chemical baths of a dimly lighted darkroom. In remote locations, photographers carried small satellite transmission dishes that connected them to their home base in a matter of minutes. In other environments, they used cell phones to transmit their pictures. Most of the pictures from the Associated Press's 1999 Pulitzer Prize series

on the Bill Clinton/Monica Lewinsky scandal were transmitted from office hallways and automobiles minutes after they were made by using digital cameras and cell phones. A picture from Desfor in Korea could take 24 or 48 hours to reach New York. In the late 1990s it might take 15 to 20 minutes. And the picture would be in color of excellent quality.

Newspaper photographers eagerly adopted these advances and soon utilized the technology either on their own or by using the facilities made available by wire services that covered the same stories. More newspapers sent their own photographers to the scene of major international stories.

Higher quality pictures delivered to newsrooms more efficiently and quickly meant that more pictures were available for use in time for deadlines. This immediacy thrust photography toward a greater role in daily print journalism.

It is a credit to the Pulitzer process that exotic datelines did not push solid hometown coverage from the Pulitzer collection. Tom Gralish received his 1986 award for a story on the local homeless in Philadelphia and Dave Peterson won in 1987 for a picture report on the troubles faced by farmers in the Midwest. And Clarence Williams won an award in 1998 for his story of drug addiction in Long Beach.

In 1987, Scott Shaw made the marvelous picture of Baby Jessica saved from a well and, with Annie Well's single picture in 1996 of a river rescue in Santa Rosa, maintained the presence among the Pulitzer winners of the single, graphic picture.

Despite technology, despite speed, despite the far-flung travels that photographers undertook to cover the world, the thread of the Pulitzer's classic standards prevailed.

Execution on the Beach

BY LARRY PRICE, THE FORT WORTH (TEXAS) *STAR-TELEGRAM*

Larry Price went to Liberia to photograph missionaries but ended up covering the final phases of a coup d'etat—the mass execution of the government's leadership.

Liberia is a country that, by African standards, has had a long, stable history. Its roots, deep in American soil, go back to slaves freed before the American Civil War who sailed to Liberia to take up a new life. These black colonials developed a ruling aristocracy that presided over the more traditional tribal populations. Inequity was deeply established in the country.

In the small hours of April 12, 1980, Master Sergeant Samuel Doe headed up a handful of enlisted men who quietly entered the presidential grounds. They killed a staff of very surprised guards, stormed the corridors of the building's posh living quarters, and shot and killed President William Tolbert. The rest of the military, who like Doe came from the oppressed class, rose up in support of the insurgents. Political prisoners who had sought to install reforms and otherwise improve the lot of 90 percent of the population were set free.

Larry Price was assigned to cover the revolution's impact on missionaries in Liberia, many of whom had studied at a Baptist divinity school in Fort Worth. He spent several days photographing schools, missionaries at work, and their lifestyle. Nearly finished with his missionary coverage, Price decided to attend a press conference, the first Doe had called some ten days after the explosive overthrow of the government. The conference was brief, but at the conclusion it was announced that executions were underway on the beach.

Nine stakes the size of telephone poles had been plunged into the sand; and, as Price arrived, 13 members of the Tolbert cabinet had completed a forced march through the streets and nine of them were being lashed to poles. Armed soldiers stood nearby. Price originally took up a position with other members of the press corps; as the soldiers took their positions, however, he moved forward and stood behind the lineup of executioners. Thousands of onlookers watched in a near carnival mood, shouting, singing, laughing. The soldiers lifted their weapons; the crowd became silent.

Tolbert's men, Price recalled, looked exhausted. None of them spoke or struggled, but silently waited the inevitable, which came in a volley of rifle fire. As if on signal, the crowd burst out in joyous

JANUARY 1980 ■ *Six Americans who evaded the embassy takeover in Tehran escape from Iran by posing as Canadian diplomats.*

FEBRUARY ■ *Speedskater Eric Heiden wins five gold medals at the Olympics in Lake Placid, New York.*

APRIL ■ *The master of suspense, Alfred Hitchcock, dies at age 80 in Los Angeles.*

MAY ■ *Mount St. Helens, a volcano in Washington State, erupts.*

TECHNICAL DETAILS   **CAMERA** Nikon and Leica
FILM Kodak
LENS Various, ranging from 20 mm
to 300 mm
SHUTTER & APERTURE Various

exclamation. The remaining ministers were taken to the stakes and
lashed in place amid the bodies of their former comrades. Another
volley echoed along the beach, and another cry erupted from the
crowd. Soldiers moved forward and, in a frenzied blood lust, emp
tied their automatic weapons into the corpses. A flying shell case
hit Price in the face. The jubilant crowd danced in the sand around
the jumbled bodies.

The only American cameraman on the scene, Price boldly
photographed it all, then left Liberia carrying his film past
airport inspectors who carefully examined all the other journalists'
baggage.

Some ten years later Sergeant Doe fell to an executioner's
bullet.

TECHNICAL DETAILS   **CAMERA** Nikon
FILM Kodacolor and Kodak black & white
LENS Various, ranging from 24 mm
to 180 mm
SHUTTER & APERTURE Various

"The doors clanged shut and I really felt free." However, his relief was shortlived. The *Free Press,* like many newspapers in the early 1980s, was just beginning to print color. Yamasaki, therefore, shot almost all black and white and only a few rolls of color film. But his editors, impressed by the color pictures, decided they would use more color with the story. They asked him to return to the prison to reshoot some material in color.

He did so, and his Pulitzer was one of the first that featured color pictures.

His story was carried as a seven-part series in the *Free Press.* In one of the stories Yamasaki wrote to go with his pictures, he quoted a guard talking about the pervasive violence and the overcrowding. The guard said that the only thing that would change the situation would be a riot. Several months later rioting broke out in the Michigan prison system.

Several years later Yamasaki left the *Free Press* and worked as a freelance photographer shooting primarily for *People* magazine covering stories as far flung as Bosnia and Nicaragua. He also taught at Michigan University's School of Art and Design, occupying the prestigious Distinguished Visiting Artist's Chair at the school.

War and Children

BY STAN GROSSFELD, *THE BOSTON GLOBE*

TECHNICAL DETAILS	
CAMERA Nikon	
FILM Kodak	
LENS Various, ranging from 18 mm to 300 mm	
SHUTTER & APERTURE Various	

There was plenty of violence to cover in Lebanon in 1983. The country was split by political, religious, and economic factors. Palestinian refugee camps that were home to guerrilla units were under constant attack by Israel. An Israeli invasion the previous year moved to the outskirts of Beirut before withdrawing under world pressure. A barracks where United States Marines on peace-keeping duty lived was blown up, killing 241. Car bombs exploded regularly, and Beirut's beachfront hotel district was in ruins. The city was a mess, beset by snipers, looters, and others passionately dedicated to their cause.

Stan Grossfeld, of the *Boston Globe*, covered his share of the war, taking pictures during firefights in Tripoli as well as in Beirut. He frequently turned his camera away from the fighting itself, however, and focused on the children of Lebanon who knew no life but that of the besieged. His purpose was to show how the war had infiltrated the childhood world of Lebanon's coming generation.

To find good picture subjects, he carefully picked his way through the city's rubble, alert for snipers, who took potshots at anything that moved in sectors of the city considered "the other side."

JANUARY **1983** ▪ *Chiang Ching, widow of Mao, has her death sentence commuted to life in prison.*

APRIL ▪ *The U.S. Embassy is bombed in Beirut, killing 63 people.*

JUNE ▪ *Sally Ride, one of a five-member crew aboard the space shuttle* Challenger, *becomes the first American woman to go into space.*

His searches were rewarded. Here and there he found children playing the games of children, just as their parents played the war games of grown-ups. There were children with hula hoops, but there were also children in panic as shells fell near their protected schools. Children rode Ferris wheels, but in the background were warships moving into place in the harbor. In one instance, Grossfeld discovered a group of children, armed with guns almost as big as they were, who had been assigned to protect younger children.

The Pulitzer Prize has frequently been awarded for photographs showing the heat of battle, or its impact on soldiers involved, but in this case it was given to a photographer who, although assigned to cover the war, had the instinct to step back and document the greater implications of the situation in Beirut.

1985 [NEWS]

The Los Angeles Olympics

BY THE STAFF OF THE *ORANGE COUNTY (CALIFORNIA) REGISTER*

The Olympic Games are a spectacle. Exotic languages from every corner of the world are spoken in a single city. Pageantry abounds. Athletes are motivated to run faster, jump higher, and throw greater distances than they do at other competitions.

The Games are a photographer's delight. With muscles rippling and faces taut with strain, the athletes push their talents to the ultimate limit. Joyous winners celebrate their victories enthusiastically; losers sometimes show their disappointment openly. Because the events are structured, photographers have the opportunity to seek camera positions that will produce pictures at once artistic and newsworthy. The smaller cameras and, more importantly, longer lenses available for recent Games offer challenging picture possibilities to the creative photographer.

The Los Angeles Olympics of 1984 was different from other games in one respect. The Soviet Union, in retaliation for an American boycott of the 1980 Moscow games, refused to participate, and most of the Eastern European nations followed suit. Still some 8,000 athletes from 140 countries gathered in a steamy Los Angeles August for two weeks of competition.

The *Orange County Register*, which is published in Santa Ana, California, assigned three staff photographers. Their goal was to cover the Games and tell the story of the winners and losers, but to give special attention to pictures that also caught the beauty of the Olympic pageant.

Rick Rickman, Hal Starzel, and Brian Smith did just that. Their combined picture portfolio told both stories—athletic achievement and the beauty of the Games.

MAY 1984 ■ *Public confidence in banks declines after the Continental Illinois Bank narrowly escapes failure.*

JULY ■ *Geraldine Ferraro is picked by Walter Mondale to be his running mate for the presidential campaign.*

JULY ■ *Miss America Vanessa Williams is forced to give up her crown due to the furor over the publication of nude photographs of her.*

OCTOBER ■ *India's Indira Ghandi is assassinated at age 66.*

TECHNICAL DETAILS   CAMERA Nikon
                     FILM Kodacolor
                     LENS Various
                     SHUTTER & APERTURE Various

Famine

BY STAN GROSSFELD, *BOSTON GLOBE*

Ethiopia was dry in 1984. Subnormal rainfall had reduced grain production for three years until it was dropping at precipitous rates, as much as 30 percent a year. The problem was not unique to Ethiopia; all of Africa was suffering as the fields once lush with crops slowly turned to dust.

The lack of food put people on the move, forcing them from their farms and villages to refugee camps that had been set up on an emergency basis. The situation was made worse by rebel activity in Ethiopia, another problem common to the African nations. Food became first the trophy of the rebel and guerrilla groups, and then became the national currency. Shipments of international aid were diverted from one side of the political spectrum to another, depending frequently upon which side controlled the highway or the warehouse involved in food shipments.

Stan Grossfeld, a Pulitzer winner of the previous year for pictures made in strife-torn Lebanon, went to Africa and provided some of the first pictures to come from rebel-held areas. This was the year that international aid officials estimated that half a million people perished from starvation.

Classic among all-time Pulitzers is his striking picture of an African madonna, holding her starving child only hours before the child perished in a refugee camp. Another photo shows a line of refugees fleeing hostilities and beginning their trek across a dusty plain bound for a refugee camp in Sudan.

These early pictures by Grossfeld were the first of several Pulitzer Prizes that showed the persistent famine problems and the brutal civil war that inevitably became woven into a fabric of politics and starvation in Africa.

TECHNICAL DETAILS   **CAMERA** Leica and Nikon
FILM Kodak
LENS Various, ranging from 24 mm to 200 mm
SHUTTER & APERTURE Various

DECEMBER ▪ *Bernard Goetz, New York City "subway vigilante," shoots four black youths on the subway after they allegedly robbed him.*

DECEMBER ▪ *A Union Carbide plant in Bhopol, India, leaks lethal gas, killing more than 2,000 people.*

Covering The Rebels

BY LARRY PRICE, THE *PHILADELPHIA INQUIRER*

Shooting pictures of rebel movements in Third World countries is a dangerous game. Larry Price of the *Philadelphia Inquirer* covered two separate rebel struggles in 1984.

Angola

High on the list of "to do" stories at the *Inquirer* was a feature on a rebel movement in Angola. Backed by the United States against the Cuban/Soviet supported central government, the well-armed rebels held about half of the country, but coverage of their activities had been light. There were problems contacting them and there would be problems getting into the country.

Price found a way, however, when he met a nurse who knew medical aid personnel working in Angola. They put him in touch with anti-government Angolan representatives in Washington; after months of conversations, the setup was arranged. Price and an *Inquirer* writer traveled to Zaire, where authorities were sympathetic to the rebels. They did not enter the country officially but embarked on an eight-hour flight in a prop plane that took them to rebel headquarters in Angola. There they joined a rebel unit in the field.

"We spent weeks," Price reported, "riding in the back of a

TECHNICAL DETAILS   **CAMERA** Nikon
FILM Kodachrome
LENS OPENING Between f8 and f11
SHUTTER SPEED 1/400th second

truck with the soldiers. The trip was supposed to last three weeks, but it went on for six. Once in, we couldn't get out when we wanted to. Our families and the people at the Inquirer wondered what happened to us."

At one point the rebel unit was pinned down in a town by Angolan air surveillance and went without water for two days, but eventually they slipped out, crossed into Zaire and returned home.

El Salvador

Coverage of rebel troops in El Salvador proved more dangerous, simply because there was much less territory for the rebel soldiers to hide in. Government troops were in better control, and at one point, an army helicopter caught Price's unit in an exposed position and attempted to wipe out the rebels with gunfire.

"We scrambled for cover under a culvert and were safe, but the greater fear was that government ground troops would be sent out to capture the rebel units," Price said, "but that didn't happen."

Both the Angola and the El Salvador stories appeared as major layouts in the *Inquirer*'s Sunday magazine.

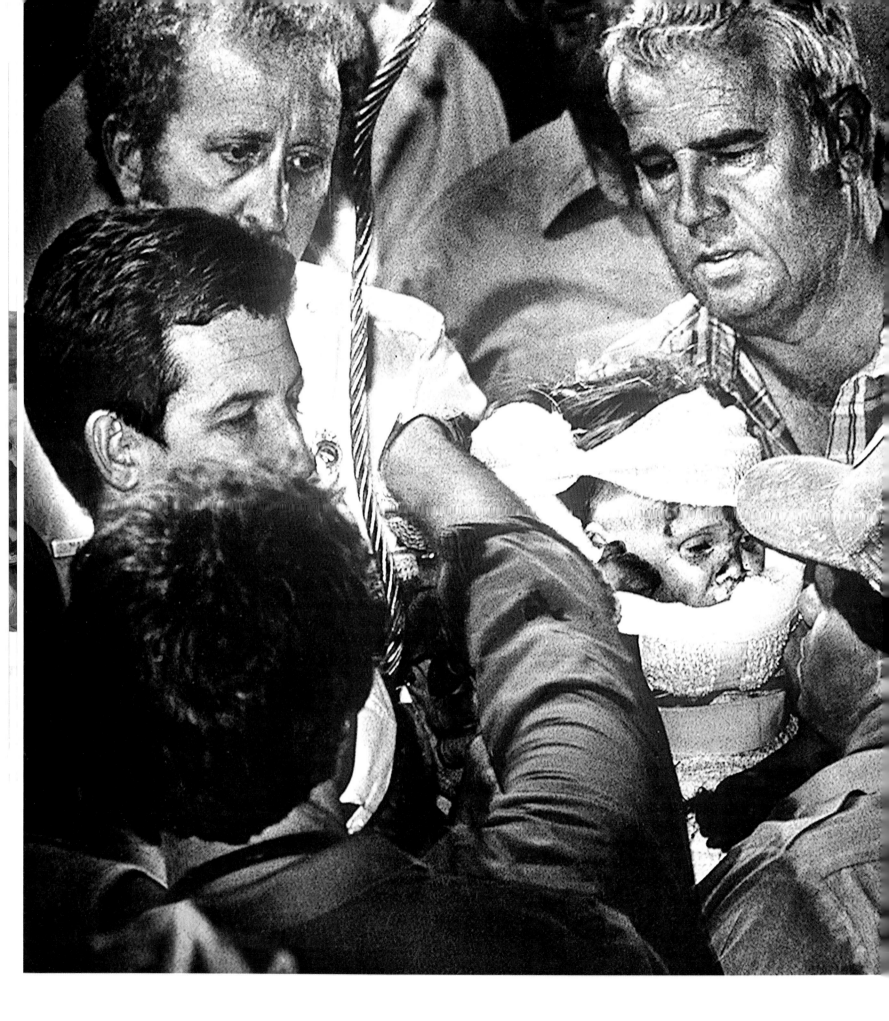

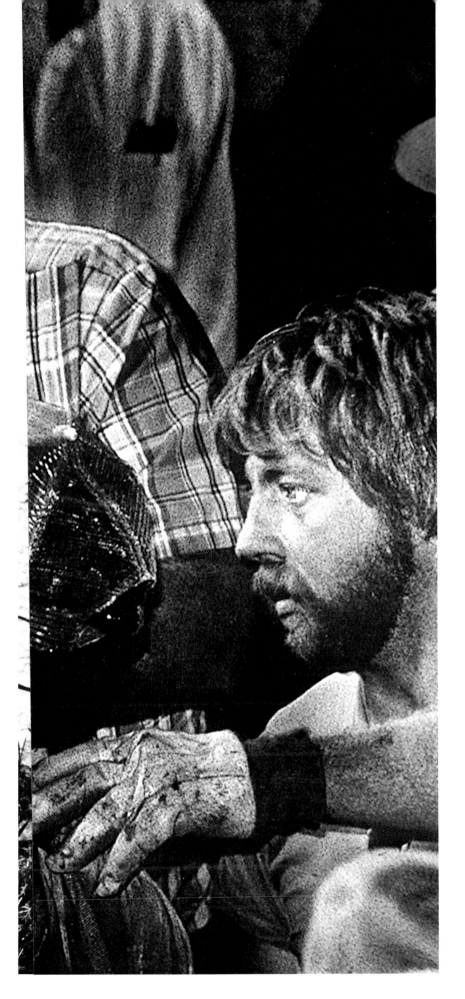

Jessica's extended plight seized the attention of the nation, and then took on global proportions. The small number of local news people was soon augmented by some 40 still photographers and a large number of television crews. Shaw kept his attention and his camera focused on the rescue operation. He borrowed a ladder from one local resident, but the man then sold it to a television photographer. A janitor who worked for the *American* lived nearby and provided Shaw with another ladder. He later moved to the bed of a cherry picker brought to the scene as part of the rescue team. Each move took him to an improved vantage point.

Some 40 hours after Jessica fell into the well, the workers bit through into the well's channel—a hole about two inches around. Water drills did the rest, patiently and slowly, until the rescuers were through. They covered the child with petroleum jelly, slid her out, and handed her up into the blazing lights of the cameras that sent their images of Jessica around the world. She was safe 58 hours after she had dropped into the well; the world breathed a sigh of relief. It was a scene of classic salvation in the Hollywood mode.

Shaw was in a semicircle of photographers poised around the rescue hole, and he shot the first rescue picture with a 180 mm lens. Others used longer lenses, up to 300 mm, but Shaw's wider, looser picture included rescue workers watching intently as Jessica, badly scratched and wrapped in bandages, was lifted out of the hole. He shot seven frames of the scene, but only one captured the intense facial expressions of every worker staring at Jessica at the moment of rescue.

The workers carried the baby across the yard to a waiting ambulance. Shaw changed lenses, attaching a 300 mm to his camera. As Jessica was quickly carried past him he shot automatically, not certain what the image would look like.

Later, in the office, exhausted from the sleepless hours waiting for Jessica's freedom, Shaw saw his long-lens photo; it was dead sharp, with Jessica's bright eyes twinkling in the light. The paper used both photos, one on the front page and one inside.

After the incident, Jessica's parents kept her out of the limelight, hoping that she would enjoy a normal childhood. Later, when ten-year anniversary stories were written, Jessica said she had no direct memory of the incident. She lost a toe and bore a few scars, but there were no other recollections save those gleaned from news reports and portrayed in a television movie entitled *Jessica: Everyone's Baby*.

Shaw left the *American* several years later and took an assignment with the *Cleveland Plain-Dealer*.

School Days

BY MANNY CRISOSTOMO, *THE DETROIT FREE PRESS*

Manny Crisostomo's idea was simple enough, but to maintain the required momentum for successful coverage from start to finish would require an unusual level of energy and sustained enthusiasm. The *Detroit Free Press* photographer wanted to document the life of high school students as they passed through a full school year.

"One of the hardest parts," he recalled, "was getting approval from the school district. But I worked with a friend of mine who knew how the bureaucracy worked and how to phrase a request. The answer came back, 'which school do you want?'" He chose a school he described as "balanced—white kids and black kids, Hispanics, middle class. I was looking for something typical."

Crisostomo knew, as did the other Pulitzer winners who undertook photo projects requiring access to the subject, that a period of letting the subject get to know you was essential. Many of the students, Crisostomo recalls, were apprehensive about reporters, photographers, and the media in general. It took time to build trust.

For the 40 weeks of the school year, Crisostomo spent three or four days a week hanging out at the school and in the neighborhood. "I met with the kids, I went to class with them, I played their games, I debated with them...and I photographed them. I even went to their dances and to their prom."

After a while, he was accepted as part of the scene and that is when the good pictures happened. It was difficult, Crisostomo recalls now, to keep personal feelings out of the story. He remembers that he developed a certain care, even a sympathy, for the students and their lives, and it would be easy to paint their lifestyle in either a negative or a positive way unconsciously. What he wanted was a truthful balance that showed reality.

By the end of the school year in June 1988, Crisostomo had a hundred pictures that he thought represented the students' life that year. Stories were written to accompany the pictures, and the entire project was published in a single large section as part of the Sunday paper.

The principal, Crisostomo recalls, hated the story, but used it successfully to win a grant for the school from a soft drink manufacturer. One student who went on to an Ivy League university wrote that Crisostomo betrayed the trust that the students showed toward him. A year later, the student wrote again to apologize for the earlier letter and to say that the story had been a true portrait of the year.

Crisostomo contributed his Pulitzer Prize money to the school for use as a scholarship. Once the word was out, his newspaper, the newspaper group, and several large corporations also contributed money. A scholarship fund of $20,000 was accumulated that provided a number of scholarships over the next four years.

Several years after winning the Pulitzer, Crisostomo returned to his native Guam, where he eventually bought and now operates a publishing business. He also began work on a book about the Chamorru, the indigenous people of the Mariana island chain.

TECHNICAL DETAILS	
	CAMERA Canon
	FILM Kodak
	LENSES 24 mm and 105 mm
	SHUTTER & APERTURE Various

1991 [NEWS]

Fiery Death in South Africa

BY GREG MARINOVICH, ASSOCIATED PRESS

TECHNICAL DETAILS	
CAMERA	Nikkormat
FILM	Fuji color negative
LENS	Zoom, 35 mm to 70 mm and 300 mm
SHUTTER & APERTURE	Various

Four white photographers who covered South Africa's violent turn from apartheid to a new form of government came to be called the "Bang-Bang Group." A South African magazine coined the name in recognition of the photographers' consistent picture coverage of the bloody, deadly clashes in the nation's black townships.

Picture-making in townships like Soweto was risky. This was where partisans of Nelson Mandela's ANC party, which was newly legalized, and the Zulu-backed party called Inkatha, fought their bloody struggles for supremacy.

Greg Marinovich, of the Associated Press, was one of the members of the Bang-Bang Group. Greg and his companions, who were both freelancers and staff photographers of Johannesburg newspapers, traveled to the townships early in the morning. They called their forays dawn patrols because trouble frequently exploded when people were on the streets heading for work. The hostels where the workers lived were the flash points of sudden, unpredictable violence.

The group traveled together—sometimes three of them, sometimes four—as a protective measure against the violence that could easily be turned against white photographers when trouble broke out. Also, as the two fighting factions battled hand to hand with rocks, knives, spears, and small arms, police often used excessive firepower to stop the outbreaks, and photographers often ended up in the crossfire.

MAY 1990 ■ Seinfeld *begins a hugely successful nine-year run on television.*

AUGUST ■ *Iraq invades Kuwait over an oil and land dispute.*

OCTOBER ■ *After 43 years of separation, East and West Germany reunite.*

NOVEMBER ■ *After 11½ years in office, Britain's Margaret Thatcher is forced out and replaced by John Major, her handpicked successor.*

On September 15, 1990, Marinovich was in Soweto watching over the work hostels where hundreds had died in the fighting of recent months. Near a train station, he noted a group of young men crouched along an embankment. They told him that Zulus on the other side had shot at them. At that moment, one of the group fired a pistol in the direction of the Zulu hostel. Other shots were fired, but it was impossible to say where they originated.

A commotion on the train platform caught Marinovich's attention. Four or five men dragged and pushed another man from the station to the street. Marinovich recalls, "The group said the man was Inkatha, a member of the rival Zulu group and a spy. I asked them how they knew. They said, 'We know.'"

They dragged the man into the street and stoned him with fist-sized rocks that knocked him down. Several attackers stabbed him in the chest with large knives. When he got up, the youths threw larger boulders at him and knocked him down again. They told Marinovich, "No pictures! No pictures!" He replied, "I'll stop making pictures when you stop killing him."

The attack continued, however. One man stepped forward and plunged a dagger into the man's head, but still, he got up and staggered in the street. More rocks. More stabs. He fell. Another man stepped forward and poured gasoline over him. A box of matches was handed around, and one person stepped forward, struck the flame, and tossed it on the injured man. The fire swept over him in

seconds. He jumped up in agony, ran in a few circles, and then fell for a final time.

AP's photo network carried the full picture series around the world in a matter of minutes, and editors at daily papers found themselves dealing with the problem they had encountered with many of the pictures that later won Pulitzer awards. Were they too grisly to publish? One survey revealed that about half the papers polled published the photo of the stabbing or of the burning, and many printed the color photos on the front page. Others said the pictures reflected extreme violence and animalistic hatred and were too tough to print.

The Pulitzer committee showed no such reluctance, however, when it awarded the Pulitzer Prize to Marinovich. The award, in fact, acted as a stamp of approval, and a group of editors and several papers that did not print the pictures when they first appeared published them with their stories on the Pulitzer announcement.

After he won the Pulitzer, Marinovich continued to cover the struggle in South Africa until he was seriously wounded while photographing a tribal clash in 1992. Another member of the Bang-Bang Group was killed in the same encounter. Marinovich later worked in Israel for AP, then left the wire service to try his hand at writing. Kevin Carter, a third member of the group, won the 1994 Pulitzer Prize for a picture from Sudan.

1991 [FEATURE]

The Irrecoverables of Romania

BY WILLIAM SNYDER,
THE *DALLAS MORNING NEWS*

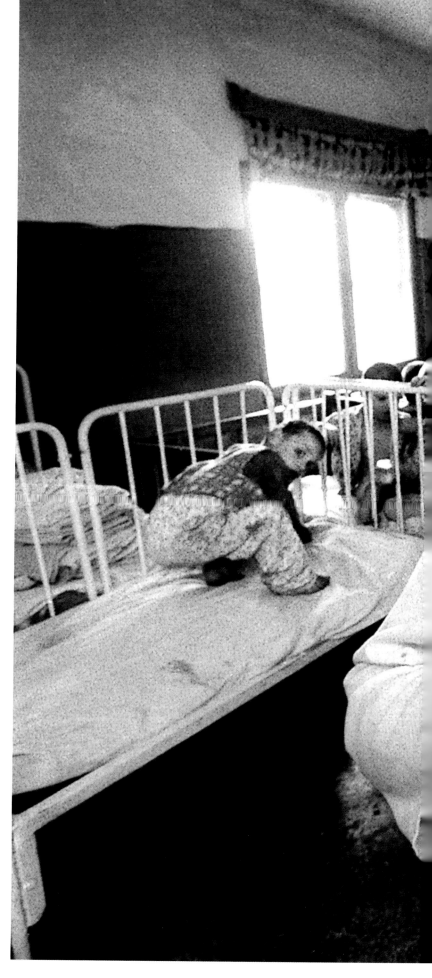

The long, harsh rule of Romanian dictator Nicolae Ceausescu was over, ended by an executioner on Christmas Day 1989. Free elections, the first in more than half a century, were scheduled for May.

In the social debris that Ceausescu left behind was a festering problem of orphaned children. Determined to build a worker force, Ceausescu had outlawed birth control for families with fewer than four children. At the same time, however, economic policies drove up living costs to the point that couples could not support a family of that size, and children were placed in state-run orphanages that themselves were understaffed. Dirty needles were used for injections, little attention was paid to babies, and diseases, including AIDS, spread rapidly.

Bill Snyder, of the *Dallas Morning News,* read a short article in the paper that briefly described the devastating problems facing Romanian orphanages, and he knew there was a story there worth doing. When he learned that election experts from Texas would act as advisors to the officials who were organizing the Romanian elections, the way was clear for him to go to Romania.

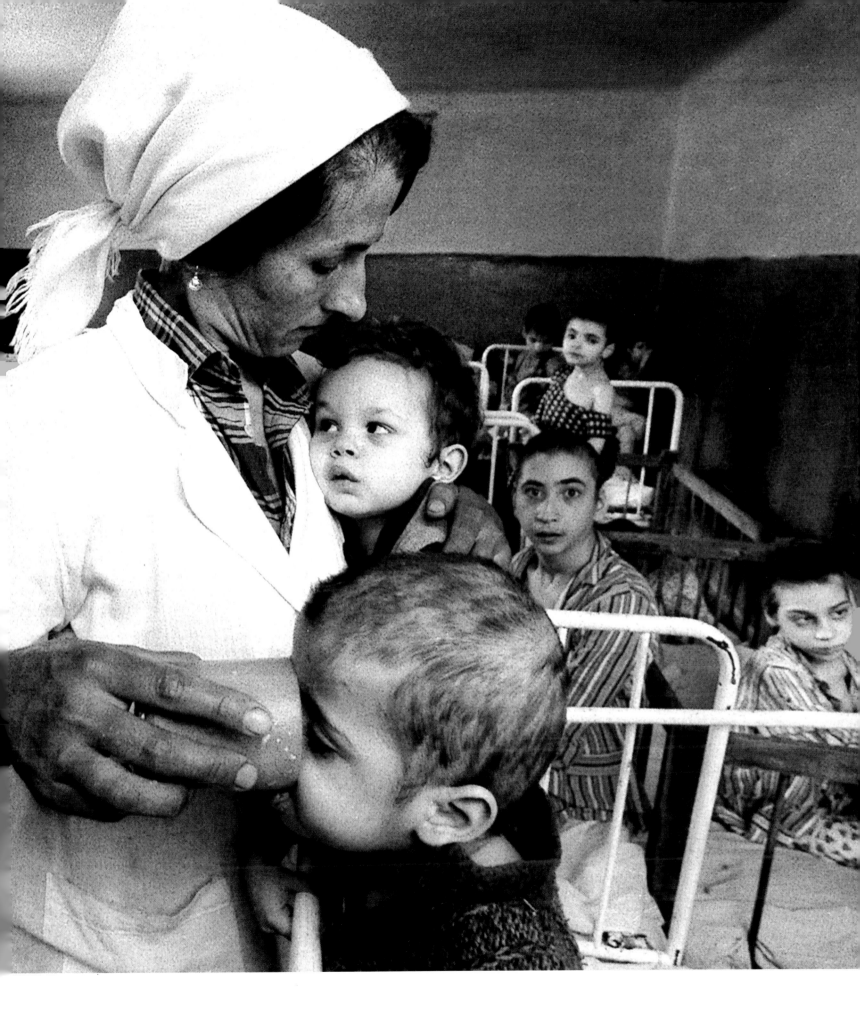

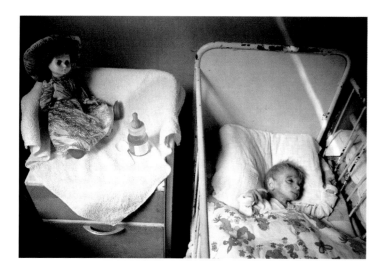

TECHNICAL DETAILS	CAMERA Nikon
	FILM Kodak color negative
	LENS Various, ranging from 20 mm
	to 180 mm
	SHUTTER & APERTURE Various

With the elections near, and with additional story ideas suggested by several *Morning News* departments, Snyder set off on his own for Romania. He would do several stories, including the elections, but the orphan story was at the top of his list.

"I was lucky in so many ways," he said. "A driver-translator I hired was able to get me into practically every place I wanted to visit, including a home for irrecoverables in Vulturesti."

Snyder's pictures captured the fate of children in several orphanages that were jammed far beyond normal capacity. In some cases, he reported, one attendant had to care for 30 infants. Malnutrition was widespread and blood transfusions done with dirty needles had spread AIDS among the children.

"These kids were not being cared for," he said, "they were being warehoused."

Snyder was the winner of three Pulitzer Prizes. In 1993, he shared the award with fellow *Morning News* photographer Ken Geiger for coverage of the Barcelona Olympics. In 1989, he shared in a Pulitzer in the Explanatory Journalism category for a series of articles on air crash investigations illustrated with his pictures.

The Death of the Soviet Union

BY THE ASSOCIATED PRESS

Life was changing at an alarming rate in the Soviet Union of 1991. As one Associated Press writer put it:

"An AP posting in Moscow always required a sense of adventure, a talent to improvise, a feel for history, and the will to endure hardship. These days, it also requires the ability to adapt to relentless revolution."

The changes began when Mikhail Gorbachev came to power in 1985 and launched *perestroika*. Four years later the Berlin Wall came down, and the Soviet bloc was in chaos. By August the Communist hardliners knew it was do or die; the scene was set for action.

The crisis reached a climax in August, 1991, when the hardliners held Gorbachev for 80 hours at his Crimean dacha. A team of five AP photographers captured the drama in Moscow and around the country.

As one remarkable photo showed, Boris Yeltsin, firebrand activist and President of the Russian Republic, went to the streets and climbed aboard a tank to urge the Russian people to take a stand against the Communist hardliners who wanted to take over the central government. The people followed Yeltsin's lead, as did much of the Russian military and KGB. Some shots were fired elsewhere in the city and three died, but a line of tanks ready at the outskirts did not move.

Russian soldiers balked at firing on tens of thousands of their countrymen who supported change.

The coup collapsed and Gorbachev returned to find street

activists standing on and alongside their trophies, the fallen and shattered statues of Lenin and others of Communism's historic elite.

AP photographers took photos of the emotional scenes in the city but it was a simple, telling picture that captured the moment of greatest historic significance. Gorbachev, under pressure from

FEBRUARY 1991 ■ *The U.S. offensive in Kuwait, named "Operation Desert Storm" begins.*

MAY ■ *Queen Elizabeth addresses U.S. Congress.*

OCTOBER ■ *Anita Hill accuses Supreme Court nominee Clarence Thomas of sexual harassment. After a series of bitter hearings, his appointment is confirmed.*

Yeltsin, agreed to dissolve the discredited Communist Party. Later, as Soviet republics seceded from the Union, Gorbachev appeared on television December 25, 1991 and resigned as president of a nation that no longer existed.

His speech completed, Gorbachev closed the file holding his prepared remarks and communism's seventy-four-year rule of Russia came to an end. AP photographer Liu Heung Shing took pictures with a camera hidden under his coat of the last moments of one of history's most dramatic sagas. Moments later the red flag of the Soviet Union was taken down from the Kremlin's highest tower.

TECHNICAL DETAILS

CAMERA Leica and Nikon
FILM Kodak color negative
LENS Various
SHUTTER & APERTURE Various

The Barcelona Olympics

BY WILLIAM SNYDER AND KEN GEIGER, THE DALLAS *MORNING NEWS*

The quadrennial Olympiad is devoted to sports and athletic achievement but, as with so many international events, nationalism and power politics get into the act. The 1992 games at Barcelona were no different. In fact, a case could be made that politics had the edge.

More than 15,000 people from 185 countries participated at Barcelona, the largest number ever. There were still, however, these political considerations: the Russians, always a power at the Olympics, entered its athletes as a joint Eastern union of 12 Soviet republics; South Africa was back after a thirty-two-year absence; North Korea and Cuba competed for the first time; and the newly re-united Germany entered a unified team. The program of the Barcelona Olympiad thus resembled a diplomatic document reflecting the political realignments that followed the end of the Cold War.

Bill Snyder, fresh from coverage in Romania that won a 1991 Pulitzer Prize, teamed up with fellow *Dallas Morning News* photographer Ken Geiger to cover the games. A few days in the sun covering sports in Barcelona sounds like one of those dream assignments that turns up a couple of times in a photographer's career, but this was not so at the Olympics, which ran from 8:00 a.m. to past midnight for 16 days straight. And it wasn't just shooting the

---

MAY 1992 ■ *After 30 years as host of* The Tonight Show, *Johnny Carson retires.*

AUGUST ■ *Hurricane Andrew, the most powerful hurricane ever to strike the continental U.S., devastates Florida.*

NOVEMBER ■ *Bill Clinton defeats George Bush in the U.S. presidential campaign, becoming the first Democrat elected president since 1976.*

DECEMBER ■ *Buckingham Palace announces that Prince Charles and Diana, Princess of Wales, have separated.*

pictures; film has to be processed, edited, and transmitted to the paper on the other side of the world.

It was a grueling, demanding task in an Olympiad that, beside politics, was said to feature the hottest weather in Olympic history. A normal day started with the swimmers or divers (shoot, process, transmit), then moved to track and field (shoot, process, transmit), and then gymnastics (shoot, process, transmit); and add a basketball game here and there, some equestrian events, and maybe water polo. An Olympiad can offer more than 20 athletic disciplines to competitors.

The two photographers, who had attended university together at the Rochester Institute of Technology, turned in a gold-medal performance on the Games and won the Pulitzer Prize. It was Snyder's third award. In addition to the Romanian coverage, he also won for his participation in an Explanatory Journalism story winner in 1989.

TECHNICAL DETAILS

CAMERA Canon
FILM Various color films
LENS Various, ranging from 200 mm to 600 mm
SHUTTER & APERTURE Various

The Clinton Presidential Election Campaign

BY ASSOCIATED PRESS

Wire services face certain inescapable requirements when they cover a presidential political campaign.

- Coverage must be complete, so frequently more than one person photographs each situation.

- The need for speed is ever present. Newspapers and other publications worldwide expect the most recent pictures by deadline.

- Competition is fierce. Scores of photographers cover the campaign, and each one seeks the unusual, the special moment, and the right angle for a photograph.

- Despite the number of cameras present and the demands of speed, photographers still search for the unique, insightful picture that others miss or do not see.

When William Jefferson Clinton pursued the U.S. presidency in 1992, the photographers assigned to the campaign faced all of these traditional challenges. In addition, campaign planners, spin meisters, and others who handled the candidate, moved him here

219

TECHNICAL DETAILS   **CAMERA** Nikon and Kodak digital camera
FILM Kodak color negative and digital
LENS Various
SHUTTER & APERTURE Various

and there—one time for a sound bite, the next time for a picture—always positioning the campaigner to maximum advantage.

Wire-service photographers call the collected daily results of their team coverage "the report." For the Associated Press photographers following Clinton, producing the report of the campaign was a blurred rush from place to place. They shot pictures quickly, and handed the film off to others who processed and edited the exposures while the photographers raced to the next photo op. It was sometimes hours, but more often days or even longer, before a photographer saw the results.

In some situations, photographers waited for hours until the candidate appeared, jealously guarding a spot on a platform that they hoped would put them in the proper position for the best picture of an encounter that might last only a few minutes. At other times, photographers searched for hours to locate a spot no competing photographers occupied in the hope that it might produce a different or telling photo.

Overall, however, the campaign climate was admirably suited to wire-service photographers. Unlike those working individually, they were supported by a network of bureaus across the country, had access to prime positions in pools, and located good positions by using teams to leapfrog the fast-moving candidate. The opportunity for unusual, thoughtful pictures was also enhanced for wire-service photographers because local staff photographers connected to the agency could be assigned the anticipated shot while the AP team sought out the chancy, offbeat pictures.

The pictures shown here from the Associated Press's winning portfolio, are accompanied by statements from the photographers that describe how their pictures came about.

Stephen Savoia

Clinton's media advisers decided to hold this press conference in a hangar at Boston's Logan Airport. They had that backdrop painted quickly. Although it was really big, inside the vast hangar it looked small. I said, "Let me shoot what the image meisters want me to see. But let me put my own spin on it." My intent was to expose the photo op and show how everyone looked like cardboard cutouts of themselves. Some people have said to me that this was an easy picture to make. Technically it was easy to make; but there were 15 or 20 other photographers there, and nobody else made that picture.

Marcy Nighswander

I was wandering around in the balcony, trying to find a spot where there wasn't already another AP photographer. I noticed Bush and Perot arguing in the background when Clinton was trying to speak. Clinton even turned around at one point to look at them. I think it was the only time in all of the television debates when all three candidates were in action at the same time. I was in the travel pool with Bush, so we packed and left right after the debate. I was so busy, I never even saw the photo until they showed me the package that won the Pulitzer.

Reed Saxon

This was relatively straightforward. Clinton opened the show (the Arsenio Hall Show) by sitting in with the band. The assistant director of the TV studio put me next to the main camera during the staging; but when Clinton played, the music stand blocked my view and cut off his hands and the instrument. At the last minute, I jumped to the other side of the TV camera. The photo became one of the signature images for the whole campaign.

Greg Gibson

We had an unusual situation in New Hampshire in that we had one photographer on the candidate and I could be a floater. I picked a booth at the market that I thought would have more news value. I happened to see this little boy sitting on the counter in this shop. His mother let me come back and get behind him. I guess he was hoping to get a chance to talk to Clinton.

"At the primary school midway between the maternity clinic and the church, a man lies prone beneath a meticulously drawn blackboard sketch of Africa, the capital of each nation listed alongside.

"A rebel commander said an estimated 1,500 to 2,000 people died in the carnage at Karumbamba. The only sign of human life in the area is a lone sentry posted roughly where the fresh air begins. When asked about the massacre the officer said, "It's happening everywhere.'"

The images by the four prize-winning photographers are each accompanied by the photographer's comments about his or her experiences photographing in the refugee camps of Rwanda and of nearby Zaire.

Jacqueline Arzt

Africa is the continent where humanity was born, but in July and August of 1994, other AP staffers and I saw it become saturated by misery and take its offspring back to the earth. As I was photographing, my eye would routinely linger in the frame to see if the person I was photographing was breathing. For me, winning the Pulitzer means that those who see these pictures will consider once

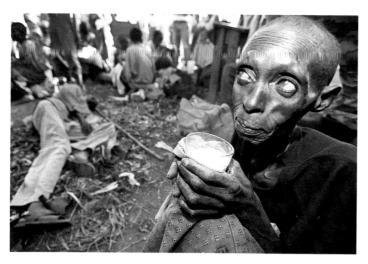

again the evil that flourishes when good men do nothing. Nearly a year later, those who have managed to survive in the refugee camps and the orphanages are still living on a prayer in a God-less land.

Javier Bauluz

I met with a photojournalist friend. We were saying that we had never seen such a terrifying thing in our lives. I heard weeping and I saw a blanket by the edge of the road. One more dead, I said to myself. Then I heard a cry from the blanket. I got closer. I unfolded the blanket and found a child maybe seven years old. Fighting the repugnance of the smell and grime, I took him in my arms and walked some 100 yards to the hospital. I left him there.

Jean-Marc Bouju

Rwanda 1994, the quickest genocide and biggest exodus in modern history. The thick smell of rotting bodies hung over the country for weeks. I think of Rwanda as a once-in-a-lifetime story. If my pictures, with the pictures and text of my colleagues, helped others to understand even a little bit the scale of the Rwanda nightmare, I am happy.

Karsten Thielker

This sickening sweet smell came from out of nowhere, we were one and a quarter miles from the scene of a three-week-old massacre. Three hundred bodies in the middle of nowhere. I was confronted with scenes that no one could ever imagine. I didn't want to send pictures of bones in dirty, bloody clothes from the church massacre, of the rotting bodies in the middle of the street. I dreaded sending pictures of these hundreds of dead, lying together as if they were still afraid to die. No one could participate in this if it were not part of covering a major story.

TECHNICAL DETAILS   CAMERA Leica and Nikon
FILM Fuji Color negative
LENS Various
SHUTTER & APERTURE Various

The Dancing Bear

BY ALEXANDER ZEMLIANICHENKO, ASSOCIATED PRESS

Politicians seeking office possess a common instinct that transcends barriers of culture and distance—each and every office seeker will do anything to get the vote. Boris Yeltsin's 1996 effort to win the hearts, if not the minds, of the Russian voter featured dancing.

He danced in Ufa as he pressed for votes and sought peace in Chechnya. He danced in Novosibirsk, Siberia, as he charged that the Communists were stirring up trouble during the election campaigns. His wife tried to pull him off the dance floor there.

Vice President Al Gore, on a visit to Russia, even complimented Yeltsin's campaign dancing during a stop in Barvikha, a Moscow suburb.

Yeltsin's political opponent, Gennady Zyuganov, tried to get on the bandwagon, as well, when he took to the dance floor in a Moscow nightclub.

But the mother of all dances was Yeltsin's vigorous performance of a tricky but unclassified number with two leggy, short-skirted performers at a rock concert in Rostov.

Associated Press photographer Alexander Zemlianichenko covered Yeltsin on many of his campaign swings across Russia and had photographed him dancing before, both with his wife, at the session at Novosibirsk, and at Ufa, where the dance was in the classic Russian mode.

Zemlianichenko's Rostov picture captured the political antics of Yeltsin, but it said even more about Russia. It told of a Russia now different than the menacing bear of the Cold War. The women dancers could be anywhere—London, Frankfurt, Rome, or New York. The white-shirted Yeltsin, tie flapping and arms askew, could be any American politician looking for a laugh that translated to votes, or any London businessman out for a night on the town. The electronic apparatus of the western rock concert added a small, but meaningful detail associated with modern music. And, best of all, the picture possessed humor, that most difficult of all emotions to capture in still photography.

Zemlianichenko took the photo in a city that would have been difficult to visit only a few years earlier. And the image showed a Russian leader quite different from Joseph Stalin, or even Mikhail Gorbachev. All these things were known, of course, but there they were, frozen in a single photo.

The picture was flashed around the world and was published on front pages from London to Tokyo, from New York to Seattle. It brought Zemlianichenko a second Pulitzer; his first was as part of the team that won the 1992 Pulitzer for its coverage of an attempted Moscow coup.

JULY **1996** ▪ *TWA flight 800 explodes over the Atlantic, just minutes after taking off from JFK airport. The cause is attributed to a fuel tank ignited by a spark.*

NOVEMBER ▪ *In an attempt at post-Cold War reconciliation, Fidel Castro meets Pope John Paul II in the Vatican.*

TECHNICAL DETAILS   **CAMERA** Nikon
FILM Fuji color negative
LENS 300 mm
SHUTTER & APERTURE Unknown

Trek of Tears

BY MARTHA RIAL, THE *PITTSBURGH POST-GAZETTE*

By and large, images awarded Pulitzer Prizes portray special moments. Sometimes they are memorable reminders of history's markers; other times they catch moments of high drama as life hangs in the balance. Occasionally they depict purely human vignettes that offer insights far beyond their specific, frozen sliver of time.

The ethnic genocide that characterized Hutu and Tutsi enmity in Central Africa of the mid-1990s held a promise of dramatic pictures that drew photographers the way a flame draws moths. The bloody and vicious events had been well documented; the pictures amply illustrated the treatment of one group by the other and showed the world what remained—orphans, widows, rape victims, and refugees. A Pulitzer had been won in 1995 for pictures of this story. Martha Rial, a staff photographer for the *Pittsburgh Post-Gazette,* sought to approach a photo essay of the social devastation from a different perspective. Rial was impressed by a conversation with her sister, a nurse assigned to the International Rescue Committee who worked in Tanzania in an area close to the Burundi border. Their exchange led Rial to seek an assignment from her paper to photograph the Hutu-Tutsi conflict through the life of the refugees that would focus on their desire to overcome adversity and find a new life. She envisioned the coverage to be presented in the form of a photographic journal that she called *Trek of Tears.*

TECHNICAL DETAILS	
	CAMERA Nikon
	FILM Color negative
	LENSES 35 mm to 300 mm
	SHUTTER & APERTURE Various

MARCH 1997 ■ *Comet Hale Bopp streaks across the sky, delighting the world with its astounding visibility.*

APRIL ■ *21 year old Tiger Woods becomes the youngest Masters Tournament winner, and sets a new tournament record with a score of 270.*

MAY ■ *In the first change of government in 18 years, Labour leader Tony Blair becomes prime minister of the U.K.*

JUNE ■ *Fashion designer Gianni Versace is murdered outside of his Miami, Florida, home.*

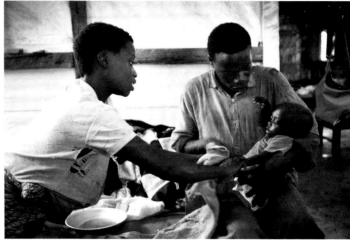

Impressed with her clear vision of the assignment, the *Post-Gazette* took the unusual step of sending one of their photographers halfway around the world.

Her pictures showed Hutu/Tutsi couples in mixed marriages who had adopted orphans to raise as their own children. She shot pictures of single women who adopted children from the other tribe. She caught the vitality of a people who had very little to live with, but who nevertheless had the spirit to live for the future. She photographed women, stabbed by bayonets and raped, who were ashamed of their scars but were willing to pose for Rial's camera in order to tell the story to the world.

Dealing with cultural differences was difficult. Rial saw men push women aside in food lines at the refugee camps. She saw a few armed military types controlling miles-long lines of refugees and wondered how the travelers could submit so easily to such harsh leadership. She was touched by the countless orphans she met who were starving for affection— some whose parents were slain in the tribal warfare, others who had lost their parents on the long flight from the war, still others who had just been abandoned.

This was not an easy assignment. Evening walks in the villages and refugee camps left Rial's eyes burning from the smoke of campfires. Her cameras and film were under constant attack from the red clay dust that permeated the atmosphere. Journeys to distant campsites were arduous and dangerous.

Rial spent three weeks in Africa shooting pictures.

The *Post-Gazette* printed 47 photos and her written journals. The passion Rial had for the story, which clearly comes through in her carefully crafted pictures, many of them artistically beautiful despite their harsh subject matter, led to her winning the 1998 Pulitzer Prize.

1998 [FEATURE]

Orphans of Addiction

BY CLARENCE WILLIAMS, THE *LOS ANGELES TIMES*

TECHNICAL DETAILS	
	CAMERA Nikon
	FILM Color negative
	LENSES 35 mm to 105 mm
	SHUTTER & APERTURE Various

Clarence Williams, a young photographer on the staff of the *Los Angeles Times,* drew the assignment to take pictures that would tell the story of the children in Long Beach, California, who live with parents addicted to drugs.

These children floundered desperately in the wake of their parents' constant pursuit of drugs. They were orphans in every meaningful sense of the word—they have little love; they have homes but little protection in a dangerous world; they live in dirt and filth, unaware that there is another way.

Williams was pleased with the assignment because, as he put it, "I see the use of drugs around me in the street, in some of my friends, even in my family." He believed his experience helped him approach the story with an open heart, and to tell it with meaning and sensitivity.

"I never felt danger in the neighborhoods where I had to go to take pictures," he said. "The only danger I felt was a fear that I would not provide the kinds of pictures that would tell the story properly and be acceptable for publication. This was an important story, and it had to be told correctly. I will do anything I have to do to make the proper pictures. It is important to bring a spiritual feeling to the photography. Even then, when you show the pictures to

JULY 1997 ■ *The British colony of Hong Kong is transferred back to communist China.*

AUGUST ■ *Diana, Princess of Wales, is killed in an automobile accident in Paris at age 36.*

SEPTEMBER ■ *Mother Teresa, the "saint of the slums" dies. She was 87 years old and had devoted her life to caring for the sick and destitute in Calcutta.*

people, you know that there are others who suffer from problems that also need telling."

Many of Williams' pictures took readers into the life of three-year-old Tamika, who toddled behind her mother as she searched for drugs. On one occasion, Tamika's mother met a friend who offered to share drugs with her. Williams went along. They entered a small shack, and Tamika's mother told her to rest. Williams saw the child lay down on a bed still wet from semen and urine while her mother shot up and smoked crack.

Williams' pictures nevertheless showed that Tamika was indomitable, running and playing and charged with energy even though, as with many children who live in a society of drugs, she had to be her own best playmate.

When the story appeared over two days in the *Times,* it forced authorities to look into the case. Tamika was placed in a foster home, and her mother entered rehab. A year later, while working on a follow-up story to the first feature, Williams took pictures at Tamika's fourth birthday party, the first birthday party the child had ever experienced, with real candles and a cake. Her mother attended, and the road ahead looked much better than the road behind. But the drug habit is hard to beat, and Tamika's mother slipped back into a life seeking speed and crack. It appeared that Tamika would be put up for adoption.

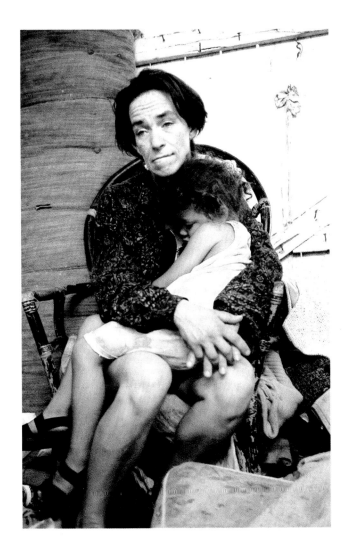

The pictures Williams took won the Pulitzer Prize, and he is pleased by the honor. It poses problems, too, because he approaches photography and photojournalism with a spiritual devotion to doing the stories correctly. "The Pulitzer pushed the standard higher," he says. "And sometimes I am disappointed because I cannot reach that height every time."

Terror Attacks at United States Embassies in Africa

BY ASSOCIATED PRESS

Terrorist attacks are most effective when they rip through the routine life of the unsuspecting and, in an instant, transform normalcy to chaos. The morning of August 7, 1998, was normal in Nairobi. Along Haile Selassie Avenue, the street that fronted the U.S. embassy in Kenya, the mid-morning crowd was building. Offices and banks were busy.

A truck drove up to the embassy gate and the driver, waving his arms, demanded entrance. Embassy guards moved forward. Shots were exchanged. Then a hand grenade was thrown.

People in modern office buildings nearby went to the window to see what happened. A bank robbery, perhaps; there were several banks in the area. Suddenly a shattering explosion drove slivers of glass into their faces with the speed of bullets. The building shook violently, then collapsed.

A sheet of fire swept across parking lots and enveloped the vehicles in nearby streets. The blast was so powerful that the bombproof doors of the embassy were blown off. In some cases, people and furniture were thrown out of buildings. Every window within a quarter-mile radius was blown out.

Just minutes later, some 500 miles away in Tanzania, a truck pulled up in front of the U.S. embassy and exploded, tearing off the whole side of the multi-story building. Seven died and 72 were injured in the area, a residential section of Dar-es-Salaam.

At the Associated Press office in Nairobi, about half a mile from the embassy, photographers Azim Sayyid and Khalil Senosi were pouring their morning coffee when the explosion shook the office. They grabbed their cameras and ran into the street.

Sayyid recalls the scene, "People were running away from the embassy. There was dirt, smoke, glass everywhere. As we came close to the embassy, we began to see bloodied people, their faces cut open. We were the first on the scene, even before the police; but already passersby who were not injured were

FEBRUARY 1998 ■ *Ethnically-charged violence breaks out in Kosovo, later leading to intervention by international forces.*

MARCH ■ *The movie* Titanic *wins 11 Academy Awards, tying* Ben Hur *for the all-time record.*

MAY ■ *Frank Sinatra, variously known as The Voice, Ol' Blue Eyes and The Chairman, dies at age 83.*

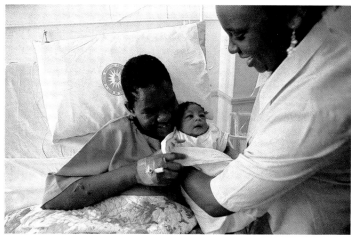

TECHNICAL DETAILS

CAMERA Nikon
FILM Color negative
LENS Various, ranging from 35 mm to 200 mm
SHUTTER & APERTURE Various

helping those who were hurt. Marine guards came out quickly and helped and tried to keep the crowd away."

Sayyid and Khalil split, one photographer went to the back of the building and one to the front. The street was littered with burned bodies and smashed vehicles. A school bus (Sayyid later learned it had stopped for a red light) was burned out, with most inside killed.

At the back of the building, Khalil watched as the wounded poured out of the embassy, and he photographed the dramatic scene of injured being passed over a broken wall on a stretcher. Nearby, the seven-story Ufundi House collapsed, killing scores of Kenyans. At Cooperative House, a tall modern structure, people were killed on each of its 21 floors. In the embassy itself, 12 Americans died.

The images left in the minds of those who were there were of charred bodies draped over buses, other bodies stacked in pickup trucks, the dazed and injured wet and stained by blood. Passing motorists took the injured to hospitals. Even the taxi-like vehicles that act as small buses and are known for their money grabbing ways pitched in to transport the wounded.

As is always the case with wire services like Associated Press, pictures must be transmitted to the world. After about 30 minutes of photography, Sayyid picked up film from Khalil and returned to the bureau, where he processed film and scanned pictures into a computer.

"My fingers were still shaking as the photos appeared on the screen and I prepared them for transmission to London and Frankfurt," he says. "They no sooner left our office than they were back on our screens, which means they had been distributed worldwide almost instantly."

Sayyid's background included both agency and newspaper work in Nairobi, but he said he had never seen anything as bloody as the scene he photographed, not even when a 747 airliner crashed before his eyes years before. This was up close and personal. Months later, Sayyid said he still jumped every time a car backfired.

The final toll at the two blast scenes—224 dead and 5,000 injured, mostly Kenyans.

Associated Press followed up on the story, covering the blast site for three weeks as rescue workers prowled through the rubble seeking first for survivors and then evidence that would identify the terrorists.

Associated Press photographer Jean-Marc Bouju, who was on the border of Rwanda and the Congo when the explosion occurred, rushed back to Nairobi. The Pulitzer-winning portfolio included his picture of Katherine Bwire, a pregnant Kenyan woman blinded by flying glass whom he photographed over several months, and who, tragically, would never see her baby.

The Clinton-Lewinsky Saga

BY ASSOCIATED PRESS

The story of President Bill Clinton and White House intern Monica Lewinsky was a classic Washington drama played out in the classic Washington manner.

Questions and answers poured forth; often the same questions received different answers. Someone lied; someone else didn't lie. That person leaked; no, that one leaked. Top administrative officials were involved, as were secretaries. The hallowed Secret Service was involved, as was the White House steward who served the coffee. The media was celebrated. The media was damned.

The entire sequence of events boggled the mind. Observers couldn't tell the players without a scorecard, and the scorecard became the pictures that appeared daily on front pages and television screens as the players rushed here and there, passing through doors enroute to meetings, hearings, or depositions in the White House, the Senate, the House of Representatives, or lawyers' offices. The players were repeatedly greeted by bursts of flashes and shouted questions as they were crushed by hordes of photographers and crowds of reporters.

All of the debate was over an ageless question—did they or didn't they? Europeans laughed at the pictures, the moralists wrung their hands; the Republicans gloated and the Democrats winced. The movie *Wag the Dog* got a boost.

JUNE 1998 ■ *Basketball great Michael Jordan, playing in his last season, leads the Bulls to their fifth NBA championship.*

JULY ■ *France wins soccer's World Cup, defeating Brazil.*

OCTOBER ■ *Slugger and first baseman Mark McGwire hits his 71st home run, setting a new record.*

Bill bit his lip and Hillary watched. Monica ran the gauntlet. The images took shape and created perceptions as they always do: Black haired, saucer-eyed Monica; harassed Bill; stoic Hillary; distressed Paula; legalistic Kenneth; ominous Linda. The pictures sorted the players out, put them in a row, and helped John Q. Public identify.

The Associated Press's problem was keeping track of it all, and making certain photographers were assigned to the proper portals and the correct hearing rooms. The photographers would wait hours for a single burst of six or eight frames of film as someone walked from a doorway to a waiting limousine. Pictures were transmitted by cell phone from digital cameras in the halls of Congress in order to meet late deadlines and match panting headlines.

At the end, and looking back, the program was complete and the players all there and properly identified.

What a show!

TECHNICAL DETAILS
CAMERA Kodak/Nikon digital camera
FILM Digital
LENS Various, ranging from 20 mm
to 300 mm
SHUTTER & APERTURE Various

ACKNOWLEDGMENTS

Special thanks and appreciation for making this book possible go to the following individuals: Lou Reda, of Reda Productions, for his persistence and moving the book from idea to reality; J. P. Leventhal, of Black Dog & Leventhal Publishers, for saying yes; Seymour Topping, of Columbia University, for his historical perspective; Patricia Lantis and Jorge Jaramillo, AP/Wide World, for making the pictures happen; John Kuss, of Corbis, for the UPI pictures; Elliane Laffont of Sygma, friend and picture provider; Vincent Alabiso, Associated Press, for guidance on AP's recent Pulitzer winners; Claudia DiMartino, for finding a mother lode; Fred Sweets, Associated Press, for making the book one hundred percent complete; Jerry Cammarata; and Angela, for patience and a lost summer.

PHOTOGRAPHY CREDITS

The time line photographs are courtesy of AP/Wide World Photos.

The Associated Press Pulitzer Prize winners are courtesy of AP/Wide World Photos.

The United Press International and David Turnley's Pulitzer Prize winning photographs are courtesy of Corbis.

Kevin Carter and Charles Porter IV's Pulitzer Prize photographs are courtesy of Sygma.

All the other Pulitzer Prize photographs are from the individual photographers and publications as indicated.

Index